the recipe for "Queue de lotte rôtie au balsamique et miel" and have at it.

At long last, dear readers, we come to *Baptism of Fire* and the fish soup that Geralt and his companions prepare and slurp down on an islet on the Yaruga River. The sheer number of times I've actually made this soup! In my kitchen at home, out in the wild, on fishing trips, on sunny days, under the stars, in rain and snow. In expensive Berghoff pots and in blackened, bubbling campfire cauldrons. I've made it from pike heads, carp, roach, perch, flounder, ruffe, North American catfish and God only knows what else. General rule: start by boiling fish trimmings in a vegetable broth. Strain that thoroughly and add the larger bits from gutting—heads, tails, fins, spines, and bones—to the strained broth. Cook it again to obtain a double broth, which you strain once more. Then add the "edible" fish bits—meaning the pieces you actually want to eat—to this strained double broth, and keep cooking to make a tripled-up soup. I'll refrain from listing specific herbs and spices, since *de gustibus* and so forth. Just season it richly and make it fiery. You may—after the Hungarian fashion—add a sizable portion of onion fried with good *édes fűszerpaprika*. I'll say it again—the soup works just as well around a campfire as it does on a table set for a holiday.

The recipe for "Redanian Fish Soup" in this book fits nicely within the canon I've delineated. Give it a try—it's worth it!

But I've digressed enough—high time to make something to eat. I think I'll try the "Fried *Kaszanka* and Egg" described in this book. I get

kaszanka (blood sausage) from my favorite store—it's the real thick Łódź-style blood sausage. Egh, I pity the nations and regions that have never known a thick Łódź *kaszanka*. They go about their lives in blissful ignorance. As for mushrooms, I have them on hand—penny buns and other boleti I forage from the Tuchola Forest and then dry. The added egg is, I admit, new to me . . . I've never had it with *kaszanka*. But it's worth trying everything you can, it's worth experimenting—after all, the kitchen is no place for pedants. So I'll go ahead and slap an egg on my blood sausage—call it a nod to the authors of this fine book.

And on that optimistic note, I'll stop. I'm grabbing *The Witcher Official Cookbook* and heading to the kitchen.

—Andrzej Sapkowski

INTRODUCTION

You might not always notice the importance of food in pop culture products, but when culinary motifs are skillfully implemented in stories, they add much more than mere decoration. The finding, making, and eating of food provides relatable insight into a given world and its culture, and into the specific characters doing the finding, making, or eating. Thanks to this, universes gain layers, depth, and believability, promoting greater immersion among the audience. Culinary themes often serve as a backdrop to stories, setting the scene for plots to develop through dialogue and intrigue, or propelling the action forward through countless tavern quarrels and fight scenes during which characters use what's at hand in combat – from cutlery, mugs, bowls, and bottles, to jars of preserve.

A large jar of cherry preserve, thought the Witcher. A jar of cherry preserve makes that noise when you throw it at somebody from a great height or with great force. He remembered it well. When he lived with Yennefer she would occasionally throw jars of preserve at him in anger. Jars she had received from clients. Yennefer had no idea how to make preserve—her magic was fallible in that respect.

Andrzej Sapkowski, "Eternal Flame"

In *The Witcher* stories—whether written on the page and brought to life in the imagination or visualized on screen—one encounters a familiar yet distorted world composed of various elements drawn from European folklore and culture. Slightly twisted versions of well-known fairy tales and legends, dropped into a fantasy setting, are a hallmark of *The Witcher*. These captivating reimaginings of classic stories we dimly remember from childhood form a rich background to the events and problems of the vivid, often morally ambiguous universe Geralt of Rivia explores.

In creating this book, we followed a similar path. Drawing guidance and inspiration from the books and games that have captivated us, we also looked to the folklore and customs of our proverbial backyard, blending them with unique *Witcher* accents and a few new topical touches of our own. We allowed ourselves a bit of freedom due to our culinary leitmotif which we emphasized not only through accurately selected and "placed" recipes, but also with fictional stories of how our narrator learned them. We found creating these short tales, limited only by our imagination, to be both a joy and a tricky task as we had to adapt our research and inspirations in tasty, entertaining ways, all the while retaining the tone of the literary source.

To tell our stories, we needed the right guide to take you on a journey through the cookbook's pages. Though we added a small sentimental surprise to the last chapter of the book, we deliberately let go of trying to step into a known character's shoes, be it Geralt or Dandelion, and having them, through their prism, lead you through the narrative. We shifted the burden of the story onto another set of shoulders.

Our narrator is a new character, a cartographer from distant Kovir with a penchant for culinary exploration. She is the ideal candidate to be our guide across the Continent, traveling as a tourist with an outlander's perspective. In this sense, she is very much like we are. Because she hasn't been involved in any known previous events, she has the freedom to simply explore these newly visited lands and engage with their inhabitants. Though it may seem as if our narrator becomes embroiled in unusual situations rather often, we believe she credibly fits into the stylings, settings, and events of the expansive *Witcher* world. For it is this world's geographic diversity that influenced our book's composition, divided as it is into chapters dedicated to specific regions, each chapter leading you through a given stage of the narrator's journey.

⎯ ⎯ ⎯ ⎯ ⎯ ◇ ⎯ ⎯ ⎯ ⎯ ⎯

The visual aspect of bringing these stories and recipes to life was equally crucial, thus we put all our passion and commitment into even the smallest

detail to reflect the specificity of *the Witcher* world for its longtime fans and to showcase it to those just discovering it. We endeavored to capture the ambiance of each place through thematic illustrations, decorative ornaments and, above all, photographs. Some of these elements refer to cultures familiar to us, be it Scandinavian accents on the frosty Skellige Isles or the charming blend of French and Italian stylings as we move into Toussaint. Naturally, the narrator's visits to White Orchard and Velen simply had to feature references to our Polish roots, represented by colorful, regional folkloric elements and Slavic accents.

⎯ ⎯ ⎯ ⎯ ⎯ ◇ ⎯ ⎯ ⎯ ⎯ ⎯

"Something Ends, Something Begins" is a fitting aphorism as our work on this cookbook comes to an end, while for you, dear reader, a culinary journey across the Continent begins. We sincerely hope that what we've produced will be warmly received as a worthy complement to the *Witcher* world. The story within strives to take you on a brief, somewhat sentimental journey. Yet you cannot fill your belly with words, so be brave and venture into your own kitchen with this book as your companion to experience for yourselves the rich, we daresay, diversity of flavors and aromas in the cuisine of the *Witcher* world.

HOW TO USE THIS BOOK

———◇———

Gaunter O'Dimm, known otherwise as the Man of Glass, proclaimed that in many matters, the culinary arts among them, time is the most important ingredient. It certainly is crucial for this cookbook. Just imagine the tempting smells of a hearty, warm, long-brewed stew served in a roadside tavern after a long journey, pleasantly appeasing your hunger and soothing the stresses of your day with each flavorful bite. So we encourage you to embrace that very concept and the carefree feeling you may get when you have a surfeit of it. Specifically, we encourage you to spend unhurried time in your kitchen enjoying the art of home cooking, and to celebrate time together over meals prepared in the *Witcher* style, with this cookbook as your companion. Here are some tips that can help you fully enjoy the culinary journey that follows in these pages.

- Whenever possible, pick high-quality, fresh ingredients from local merchants at the farmers' market and good butcher shops in your area.

- When using packaged products, read ingredient lists and choose the options that contain more natural ingredients, such as kielbasa with high meat content.

- Avoid making several shopping expeditions each time you want to try new recipes by keeping on hand basic pantry ingredients that you can store for longer. We have in mind such things as dried herbs and spices, nuts, dried fruits, dried mushrooms, honey, apple cider vinegar, groats, oils, and flours.

- Many of our recipes are inspired by European cuisine and Polish cooking traditions, with ingredients that might be easy enough to find on the Continent but may be less common in your world. Most of these ingredients can be ordered online or found at specialized European delis or natural food markets.

- Fresh herbs, especially dill and parsley, are best. As is fresh garlic. Extend the freshness of unused or extra herbs by storing as follows: sprinkle a doubled-up paper towel with water and wrap it around the fresh herbs. Put the wrapped herbs into a plastic bag, seal it, and refrigerate for up to two weeks.

- Use white onions unless otherwise specified.

- Use starchy, round potatoes rather than russet potatoes, which vary widely in size and shape.

- Use all-purpose flour unless otherwise specified. Don't use self-rising flour.

- Some dishes or ingredients are traditionally fried in lard, which gives a rich, deep flavor, but you can substitute a neutral vegetable oil (like rapeseed or sunflower) for frying if you prefer the taste.

- It's fine to use ground spices in most cases, but we highly recommend using fresh, coarsely ground black pepper and freshly grated nutmeg instead of the finely-ground packaged versions.

- Whenever milk is called for, you can substitute your preferred lactose-free or unsweetened plant-based variety.

- Most of the recipes in this cookbook require only basic equipment you probably already have in your kitchen. Sometimes we call for more uncommon equipment such as a potato masher, grater, fine-mesh strainer, whisk, tongs, wire rack, mortar and pestle (or you can use a food processor instead), basting or pastry brush, or ovenproof dish with lid. Although not available on the Continent, we also mention some modern conveniences such as electric ovens, aluminum foil, and plastic wrap.

- The recipes in this book focus on making dishes from scratch. Some preparations require advance planning and patience, but most are not too labor-intensive. Don't feel discouraged when marinating, fermenting, simmering, or proofing dough is called for—be bold and give them a go! For the times when you need faster results, it's fine to use store-bought workarounds such as broth, pie crust, or pizza dough (for recipes that use yeast-based doughs).

- Good kitchen hygiene is essential. Use separate cutting boards for raw meats and clean them afterward with hot water. To sterilize jars for brining cucumbers or making sourdough, thoroughly wash lids and jars with dishwashing liquid and rinse with hot running water. Then place the jars and lids inside a large pot to prevent splashing or spilling, and pour boiling water over the lids and inside each jar twice. Use heatproof tongs to remove the lids and jars. Set them aside until they're fully dry.

- If you see mold on brined ingredients or sourdough, discard promptly and produce a new batch.

- Our recipes call for fresh yeast but we have also provided conversions for instant yeast. You can proceed as you normally would with fresh yeast if this is what you choose.

- Store unused fresh yeast in the freezer. Crumble the yeast into an airtight container, cover, and freeze. When needed, measure the required amount of frozen crumbled yeast into a bowl and let sit at room temperature until thawed.

- When using flour, pay attention to hydration levels and refer to visual cues as per the instructions to make sure your dough has the right consistency. You can add more water if the dough is too dry or sprinkle in more flour if the dough is too moist.

- Don't waste any leftovers! For example, you can always throw some extra vegetables into any stew or use discarded leek parts to make a broth.

- Treat our recipes as guidance rather than as a strict set of rules. And remember to trust your senses. Following our tested recipes will give consistent results, but variations in the size or amount of any ingredients, the type of pan, stove, or oven, and other factors may slightly affect your results.

- We provide visual cues and photos for reference so that you can adjust heat and cooking times to get the desired level of browning, properly cooked meat, and tender but not overdone veggies; adjust the thickness of stews and soups by adding more water or broth to thin them, or simmering without a lid to thicken; adjust the balance of sour and sweet tastes to your liking by using more or less salt, spices, acids, or sweeteners.

KITCHEN SECRETS:
A TREASURE WORTH SHARING

The Continent is a colorful and intricate mosaic of lands, with the numerous variations and shades of its smaller parts combining to create an impressive pattern. It reminds me of a vibrant kitchen—of intermingling tastes and intertwining smells, braided as cultures are across regions and localities in everyday life.

Every country has its customs, and every family has its traditions. Once upon a time, my relatives began regularly collecting kitchen notes—about all sorts of dishes, from simple home recipes to those learned on journeys to far-off lands. Over many years, these loose pages turned into a bulging volume full of culinary family secrets handed down from generation to generation, a trove of priceless wealth holding traces of the past, present, and possibly the future—so, a kind of eternity. It has always been a sentimental keepsake for me, a connection to the heart of my home: the kitchen and the family table there. This kitchen table—thick and solid, made from sturdy oak, equipped with drawers and compartments—may be a bit worn and a little cracked across its surface, but it has been a faithful family companion through everyday meals and evening feasts alike. It's an enchanted place where we are transported to various corners of the Continent . . . both by tales languidly told and the flavors and smells of the dishes in our recipe collection.

There was some space left in our family cookbook—empty pages waiting to be filled with new recipes, ingredients, and culinary stories from beyond the environs of my home in Kovir. Until recently, I could only explore the world with the help of my family's abundant library of maps or my beloved books and volumes of poetry. My favorite among them has always been *The Blue Pearl* by Essi "Oeillet" Daven—I draw inspiration from the author's beautifully written ballads, and her daring character gives me courage when I face the unknown. This would very much be so when it came time for me to step across my home's doorstep and open a new chapter in the family cookbook for my own journey—a story that I would not have believed possible not long before.

For there came a day when our mapmaking workshop received a commission . . . straight from the ducal court of Toussaint, no less! We were to enrich the palace walls there with a tasteful rendering of the known world. There was nothing extraordinary about this in itself; for years, we have been sought out for the meticulous work we produce in our atelier. Occasionally, our expert drafters travel by merchant ship or caravan to clients' elegant halls and chambers to produce their intricate handicrafts on the spot. Yet for the first time, I was entrusted with representing the family and so accepted this invitation to travel due south—from our workshop in Lan Exeter to the palace halls in Beauclair.

At dawn, I boarded a merchant ship in Kovir and crossed the salty sea waves under fluttering sails. Arriving in the bustling port of Novigrad, however, I did not transfer to a vessel that would take me immediately to Beauclair, I simply could not deny myself the pleasure of visiting relatives who have lived within Vizima's walls for years. Nor could I forego the opportunity to extend my journey by several weeks with a view to exploring the neighboring lands and beyond . . . Places I had hitherto known only from family tales, the details of which I had chiefly imagined, now lay before me as stops along my journey. I set out to taste new flavors and experience life in every town, village, and tavern I would have the good fortune to visit. I resolved that no mishaps nor even fateful surprises would make me stray from my chosen course, even were it to lead me to where the devil says goodnight. . . .

So I followed a trail of delicious foods around the Continent. As my grandpapa is wont to say, the proof of the pudding is in the eating. Rest assured, I did so with gusto, be it along the sandy tracks of the Northern Realms or on the Skelige Isles' frosty, windy shores. And, eventually, indeed, in Toussaint's sun-warmed valleys, at once verdant and golden, amidst the fairy-tale beauty that reigns there.

Though ingredients and recipes were without a doubt my chief interest throughout my journey, the culinary arts draw folk of all sorts. Thus, I also gathered, or at times just overheard, the stories, gossip, and rumors of those who dined beside me. They were travelers and local folk—from fatigued royal messengers and dignified officials, through halfling scholars, carefree bards, and dwarven merchants, to even the occasional assimilated elf. And if innkeepers are to be believed in the rumors they proffer, their patrons at times included more mysterious figures oft concealed beneath hoods— mages, sorceresses, or the monster slayers known as witchers. . . .

Before I embarked on my journey, I had longed to learn what lay hidden in cellars and pantries across the Continent, and to know the delicacies served at the great feasts of distinguished hosts. I had longed to discover ingenious blends of flavors prevailing in bowls and to see hearty meals displayed on serving platters.

To satisfy these longings I needed but a bit of courage. Having found this, I went on to enjoy the culinary wonders of distant lands and to discover with my own palate positively captivating recipes offering flavorful surprises.

Previously hidden in far-away corners of the world, I have brought them home. Carefully recorded in my journal, I share these secrets now from my beloved family's kitchen.

CULINARY TRAVELS
ACROSS
THE CONTINENT

Lan Exeter

Kovir

Raer Morhen?

Novigrad
Oxenfurt

Vizima

Velen

White
Orchard

Skellige
Isles

Toussaint

Beauclair

WHITE ORCHARD

Dusty roads made moist by spring rains . . . thatched-roof huts amidst milky-white tree crowns . . . a corner of Temeria, not far from Vizima, at once quiet, quaint and strangely majestic. Those who live there call it "White Orchard" in a simple yet elegant tribute to the abundance of blossoming trees and flowering shrubs. This abundance influences the area's cuisine and has helped it rise to prominence. For a taste of White Orchard's distinctive fare, one need only cross the threshold of the hamlet's lone inn—as all passing travelers do. The ways of rural life ought never to be underestimated, and trusting one's nose is crucial. My own followed the intoxicating scent of flowers and aroma of freshly baked goods . . . The innkeeps lack expensive, exotic spices, yet they produce unforgettable meals using just local ingredients. As the harvested crops change with the seasons, so too do the specialties served. It's a rhythm as languid and unhurried as the flow of the Ismena River passing over the mill's rickety water wheel . . .

Chicken Sandwiches
with Kaedweni Stout Marinade

Weaving lazily between tables, benches, posts, and beams, the aroma of freshly baked bread was too alluring for this adventuring gourmand to resist. Arms and hands covered in flour, the cook behind the counter rattled off a list of dishes. There was no doubt as to what I would try first. This simple yet satisfying meal's creator believed near anything could be a sandwich when wedged between two generous slices of bread. In this version—a White Orchard specialty—the chicken is marinated in stout, then topped with grilled mushrooms, kale, and a mild sauce. At royal banquets and nobles' feasts, we eagerly listen to bards relating stories of old—of heroes and heroines in whose footsteps we sometimes unwittingly follow. Fabled local flavors such as this dish truly deserve ballads of their own.

—◄ MAKES 4 SERVINGS ►—

KAEDWENI STOUT MARINADE
1 cup / 240ml stout or other dark beer
2 tsp spicy mustard
1 tsp apple cider vinegar or lemon juice
2 garlic cloves, peeled and crushed
1 tsp kosher salt
1 Tbsp floral honey
—
2 boneless, skinless chicken breasts
  (about 8½ oz / 250g each)

SOUR CREAM–MAYO
¼ cup mayonnaise
2 Tbsp sour cream
¼ cup / 15g finely chopped flat-leaf parsley
Kosher salt and freshly ground black pepper
—
3 oz / 80g kale leaves, stems and midribs removed
Vegetable oil for frying
Kosher salt and freshly ground black pepper
1 tsp unsalted butter
3½ oz / 100g button mushrooms, thinly sliced
8 slices rustic bread

TO MAKE THE MARINADE: In a medium saucepan, combine the stout, mustard, vinegar or lemon juice, garlic, and salt and mix thoroughly with a spoon. Set over medium-high heat and cook until reduced to ¼ cup / 60ml and the mixture is the consistency of liquid honey, about 15 minutes. Turn off the heat, stir in the honey, and set aside to cool to room temperature.

Cut each chicken breast horizontally into two cutlets. Add the meat to the marinade, turn to coat, cover, and refrigerate for up to 1 hour. Before cooking, let the marinated chicken sit at room temperature for 15 to 30 minutes to take off the chill.

TO MAKE THE SOUR CREAM–MAYO: Meanwhile, in a medium bowl, combine the mayonnaise, sour cream, parsley, and a pinch each of salt and pepper. Stir, cover, and transfer to the fridge.

Bring a small saucepan half full of water to a boil over high heat. Turn off the heat, add the kale, and let sit for 1 minute. Then drain and set aside.

Recipe continues

In a large nonstick skillet over medium-high heat, warm 2 Tbsp vegetable oil. Add the kale and a pinch of salt and pepper and cook, stirring occasionally, until the kale is browned at its edges, about 5 minutes. Remove the kale from the skillet and transfer to a plate. Warm another 2 Tbsp vegetable oil in the same skillet. Remove the chicken from the marinade, reserving the marinade, and add to the skillet. Fry, without turning, until browned, about 1 minute. Then, using tongs, flip to the other side and cook for 1 minute more. Spread the reserved marinade on the chicken, add a splash of water, and shake the pan, then cover with a lid, turn the heat to medium-low, and cook, flipping the chicken twice, until the meat is no longer pink inside (slice with a knife to check) and well browned, about 3 minutes. Uncover, turn the heat to medium-high, and sear, flipping the chicken twice, until each side is heavily browned, 1 to 2 minutes more. Remove from the heat, transfer to a plate, cover, and set aside.

In the same skillet over medium-high heat, melt the butter. Arrange the mushrooms in a single layer and sear undisturbed until nicely browned, about 2 minutes on each side, then season with salt and pepper. Remove the mushrooms from the skillet, transfer to the plate with the chicken, cover, and set aside.

Turn the heat to medium-high, and add the bread, a few slices at a time, to the same skillet. Toast until lightly browned, about 30 seconds on each side.

Spread the sauce on each slice of toasted bread and add the kale, mushrooms, and chicken to four of the slices. Top with the remaining bread slices and lightly press each sandwich with your hand (to make it more convenient to eat) before serving.

Temerian Sourdough Multiseed Bread

While in White Orchard, I slept in an attic once used to store old junk and sacks of flour and grain. The enterprising innkeepers glimpsed an opportunity and converted the attic from a rarely entered storage space into humble yet cozy lodgings. Through the aged floorboards, the sounds and aromas of evening feasts rose up from the dining room below—the soothing scent of fresh bread serving as ample compensation for the noisy revelry and drunken carousing. The loaves were nested in baskets on the tables. The crackle of their warm crusts as they were sliced or broken became part of my daily routine. Though I was a stranger to the locals, as a guest I was granted leave to ask curiously specific questions. Soon I had learned and noted down the inn's baking secrets, including all the vital steps required to form and bake a perfect, seeded sourdough loaf.

◄— MAKES 1 LOAF —►

SOURDOUGH STARTER
1¾ cup / 210g dark rye flour, or as needed
1 cup / 240ml boiled water, cooled to
    lukewarm, or as needed

SEED MIX
1½ tsp flaxseeds
1 Tbsp chopped sunflower seeds
1 Tbsp chopped pumpkin seeds
—
2½ cups / 340g all-purpose flour, plus more for sprinkling
½ cup / 60g dark rye flour
1¼ cups / 300ml lukewarm water
1½ tsp kosher salt

TO MAKE THE STARTER: In a sterile jar, using a perfectly clean wooden spoon, stir together ¼ cup / 30g of the rye flour and 3 Tbsp of the water; the mixture should have the consistency of thick cream. Add a splash of water if the starter is too thick to stir easily. Loosely cover the jar with a kitchen towel and set aside in a dark place at room temperature for 24 hours. Repeat for the next 5 days, stirring in another ¼ cup / 30g rye flour and 3 Tbsp water each day and discarding 2 Tbsp of starter every 4 days so your container doesn't overflow. The starter should smell sour and produce bubbles after a few days. After 7 days, it is ready to use (see Note).

Every four days, transfer the sourdough into a fresh, sterile jar to avoid mold formation. If you want to store the starter, cover with a cloth and place in the fridge. While storing, feed it once a week with ¼ cup / 30g rye flour and 3 Tbsp water. (If you've forgotten to feed the starter after 7 days, make sure there's no mold on it and try to revive it by adding ¼ cup / 30g rye flour and 3 Tbsp water. However, if there's mold or if it smells bad, you must throw it away and start again.)

Several hours before you're ready to bake, add ¼ cup / 30g rye flour and 3 Tbsp water, and set aside at room temperature until doubled in size and very bubbly.

TO MAKE THE SEED MIX: Meanwhile, in a small bowl, stir together the flaxseeds, sunflower seeds, and pumpkin seeds. Add enough water to cover the seeds and set aside until the water is fully absorbed.

TO MAKE THE BREAD DOUGH: In a medium bowl, place the all-purpose flour, rye flour, and water and, using a fork, stir to combine. Cover and let sit for 45 minutes. Add ⅓ cup / 100g of the sourdough starter, salt, and a sprinkling of flour, and briefly knead the dough inside the bowl until uniform but still sticky. Cover with a kitchen towel and set aside at room temperature for 30 minutes.

Sprinkle the seed mix over the dough. Wet your hands with lukewarm water and stretch the dough by holding one end and pulling the other slightly upward, and then fold the ends inward in a motion that is similar to the way you would fold a kitchen towel. Rotate the bowl 90 degrees and repeat this motion a total of five times. Set the dough aside for 30 minutes and then repeat this process four times, covering with the kitchen towel and letting rest for 30 minutes after each stretching. The seed mix should be fully incorporated and the dough should slightly increase its volume and get fluffy and smooth in the process. Cover the bowl and set it aside at room temperature until the dough doubles in size; this should take 4 to 5 hours.

Line a proofing basket or a colander with a linen kitchen towel and generously sprinkle it with all-purpose flour.

Once the dough has doubled in size, turn the dough onto a floured work surface and fold a few times as instructed previously. Shape the dough into an oval, sprinkle both sides generously with all-purpose flour, and transfer to the prepared proofing basket or colander. Cover and set aside until doubled in size, about 3 hours at room temperature or in the fridge for 12 hours.

Place a lidded, ovenproof dish, such as a Dutch oven, inside the oven and preheat to 450°F / 240°C.

Gently remove the dough from the basket and transfer to a piece of parchment paper. Using a sharp knife or a razor blade, lightly score the dough down the middle. Transfer the dough and parchment paper to the preheated ovenproof dish, cover, and put in the oven. Bake for 20 minutes, then turn the oven temperature to 400°F / 200°C, remove the lid, and bake until the crust is well browned, 35 to 40 minutes more. Turn off the oven, slightly open the door, and let the bread sit for 15 minutes. Remove the bread from the oven, place it on a wire rack, and let cool for 2 hours before slicing.

Store the bread, wrapped in a linen cloth or a kitchen towel, at room temperature for up to 4 days.

NOTE: The starter can be used after 7 days, but younger starter results in a denser loaf when baked. If you prefer a more open loaf, continue to feed your starter as instructed.

White Orchard Inn Groats with Bacon

The White Orchard Inn is the village's beating heart and the first stop for any who seek a hearty meal and a relaxing way to pass the time. After a few days of settling in, I had to admit that my relatives in Vizima had been right to recommend it as the best place to embark on my culinary journey. One night, it seemed that nearly the whole village had gathered in its bustling main room to feast and enjoy music provided by a recently arrived Cidarian bard (a rare honor for such a humble setting). While waiting for the performance to resume, I couldn't refuse the generous offer of a portion of groats with bacon that smelled of garlic and freshly ground pepper. This simple dish, though widely known from Arcsea to Cintra, was served not only with crackling lardons, but also roasted greens.

MAKES 4 SERVINGS

3½ oz / 100g kale leaves, stems and midribs removed
1 cup / 200g pearl barley
2 cups / 480ml water
Kosher salt
5 oz / 150g slab bacon, diced
3 garlic cloves, minced
Freshly ground black pepper

Bring a kettle of water to a boil. Place the kale leaves in a sieve, pour in the boiling water, and then coarsely chop and set aside.

Put the barley in the sieve, rinse with cold water, and then transfer to a small saucepan over high heat. Add the 2 cups / 480ml of water and ¾ tsp salt, stir, cover, and bring to a boil. Turn the heat to low and cook for 15 minutes. Turn off the heat, stir, cover again, and set aside until the barley is slightly chewy yet tender, 10 to 15 minutes. The grains should soak up all the water in the process; if not, drain them.

In a large nonstick skillet over medium heat, combine the bacon and a splash of cold water. Cook until the water evaporates, about 3 minutes, then continue cooking, stirring occasionally, until slightly browned, about 5 minutes more. Add the kale and cook, stirring occasionally, until the leaves are slightly browned on the edges, 5 to 7 minutes. Add the garlic and cook for 1 minute more.

Add the barley to the skillet, season with pepper, stir until well combined, and stir-fry for 3 minutes more. Season with more salt if needed.

Transfer the groats into individual bowls and serve immediately.

Orchardman's Refreshing Nectar

White Orchard is not only famed for its flowering trees, but also for the fruit that issues in bushels from the blooms. The inn's owners directed me to the local orchard keepers, who graciously taught me this simple recipe for a refreshing libation. These masters of all things fruity work out of a hut that sits at the end of a sandy path lined by fragrant lilacs—though a quarrelsome cat that guards the way. According to the local folk, so fearless is this stubborn feline that it will not budge even for passing chorts, rumored to inhabit the nearby wood. At the end of this pleasant walk, I was rewarded with a mug of this famed beverage, made from tart gooseberries, currants, sweet cherries, and a pinch of fresh mint. The orchard keepers shared numerous recipes featuring their beloved fruit while waxing lyrical about the seasonal enemies of White Orchard's blooming period—cheeky roe deer fond of gnawing on young branches as well as so-called "cold gardeners," or frost spirits, who roam the land around the holiday of *Belleteyn*.

◄ MAKES ABOUT 8 CUPS / 2L ►

10½ oz / 300g gooseberries
14 oz / 400g sweet cherries
10½ oz / 300g red currants (see Note)
5 cups / 1.2L water, or as needed
2 Tbsp granulated sugar
2 mint sprigs (optional)
Floral honey or granulated sugar for sweetening (optional)

Wash the gooseberries, cherries, and currants thoroughly under running water. Remove the gooseberry stems and black tips, the cherry stems and seeds, and the currant stalks.

In a medium saucepan over high heat, combine the fruits, water, and sugar. Bring the mixture to a boil, and then turn the heat to low and let simmer for 5 minutes. Turn off the heat, add the mint (if using), and let sit for 10 minutes.

Transfer the mixture to a large pitcher. Taste and then sweeten the drink with sugar or honey or add more water if needed to dilute.

Serve the refreshment chilled or lukewarm, being sure to include the fruits.

Store, covered, in the fridge for up to 2 days.

NOTES

If red currants are difficult to find or are not in season, use another tart red fruit, such as sour cherries.

For a hint of floral sweetness, you can add a splash of elderflower syrup instead of the additional sugar or honey.

Willoughby Roast Chicken
with Nuts and Herbs

Willoughby, a neighboring hamlet, lies just the other side of a bridge one must cross to reach an old fortress. This once was home to a cruel baron, yet when passing villagers stop in the shadows of the castle's remains to rest and share gossip, it is not the area's former lord they speak of in hushed tones, but rather his late chef. The cook is said to have died a gruesome death and to this very day apparently lurks within the ruins during the Buck Moon (what locals call a full moon after *Midaëte* in the month of July). Rumor has it that on these nights one can hear the clatter of pots and the sound of many a plate being smashed. Folk wonder why the ghost still lingers—does he guard a treasure or hunger for revenge? None have ever plucked up the courage to investigate. Nevertheless, the phantom left behind a culinary heritage that has taken root in the village's memory. His recipe for roasted, succulent chicken with nuts and herbs was once the signature dish of every feast at Amavet Fortress and on special occasions now reigns supreme atop villagers' dining tables.

MAKES 4 TO 6 SERVINGS

3 garlic cloves, chopped
3 tsp kosher salt
3 tsp parsley flakes
3 tsp dried lovage
1 tsp freshly ground black pepper
1 Tbsp Herbal Pepper (recipe follows)
—
1 whole farm-raised chicken (about 4½ lb / 2kg)
2 Tbsp unsalted butter at room temperature

STUFFING
½ cup / 50g mixed nuts (such as walnuts and hazelnuts)
½ cup / 60g dried bread crumbs
2 Tbsp unsalted butter, at room temperature, diced
¼ cup / 15g chopped fresh flat-leaf parsley
½ tsp kosher salt
2 Tbsp cold water, or as needed
—
Vegetable oil

In a mortar with a pestle or small bowl, use a fork to mash together the garlic, salt, parsley flakes, lovage, black pepper, and herbal pepper to a smooth paste.

If necessary, remove the giblets from the chicken. Pat the chicken dry with paper towels, and then thoroughly rub the chicken skin, on each side, with two-thirds of the spice mix.

In the mortar with the remaining one-third of the garlic-herb mixture, add the butter and, using a fork, incorporate thoroughly. Carefully insert your fingers underneath the end of the breast skin to separate it from the meat. Then smear the butter mixture between each breast and its skin.

Recipe continues

Transfer the chicken, uncovered, to a plate, and then place in the refrigerator for 10 hours. About 1 hour before baking, remove the chicken from the fridge and set aside at room temperature.

TO MAKE THE STUFFING: In a dry, medium nonstick skillet over medium heat, toast the nuts, shaking the skillet a few times, until slightly browned, 3 to 4 minutes. Transfer the nuts to a cutting board, let cool to room temperature, and then mince.

In a medium bowl, combine the bread crumbs and butter and whisk with a fork until fluffy. Then add the nuts, parsley, salt, and water and stir to combine. The stuffing mixture should be moist but not runny; add a little more water if it is too dry.

Spoon the stuffing into the chicken's cavity and press with your fingers. Cross the drumsticks and bind them with kitchen twine. Then lightly fold the chicken wings behind the back of the chicken to prevent them from burning.

Preheat the oven to 400°F / 200°C. Drizzle a little vegetable oil into an ovenproof baking dish or cast-iron skillet.

Transfer the chicken to the prepared cooking vessel, place in the oven, and roast for 15 minutes. Then lower the oven temperature to 350°F / 180°C and roast until golden brown, for 70 to 90 minutes more. After the first 45 minutes, baste the chicken with its cooking juices every 15 minutes. At the end of baking, turn the oven temperature to 425°F / 220°C and roast until the skin is nicely browned and crispy, about 10 minutes more.

Remove the chicken from the oven and let rest for 15 minutes. Using a sharp knife, divide it into thighs, drumsticks, breast meat, and wings. Remove the stuffing and serve on the side of each portion. Use the remaining cooking juices to drizzle over the meat and serve immediately.

HERBAL PEPPER
Makes 1 Tbsp

1 tsp coriander seeds
1 tsp yellow mustard seeds
½ tsp dried marjoram
½ tsp caraway seeds

In a mortar, add the coriander, mustard, marjoram, and caraway and crush with a pestle until the spices are powdered and well-combined.

Miller's Bigos
Cabbage Stew with Apples and Dried Plums

This haphazard, chaotic, yet ultimately satisfying dish is a testament to the day I happened to spend on the other side of the Ismena River. To learn yet more about the local cuisine, I volunteered to assist with preparations for a food and drinks festival during which Viziman Champion beer was to flow without end. Suddenly, a rapidly approaching storm forced us to take shelter within the miller's home, where we hurriedly covered all mirrors with cloth so as not to glimpse an apparition or other terrifying spirit summoned by the tempest. The fresh, damp air mingled with the irresistible aromas of a bubbling cabbage stew with dried plums and apples and of bread baked from newly milled flour. The miller's cheerful wife served us this nourishing dish, consisting of local fruit mixed with sauerkraut, tender meat, earthy forest mushrooms, and pungent spices. As we greedily wolfed down our meal, she reminded us that the stew's flavor improves each time it is reheated, its flavors blending ever more deeply.

MAKES 6 SERVINGS

1 oz / 30g dried mushroom slices
   (such as bay bolete or porcini)
2¾ oz / 80g dried plums (pitted prunes)
3½ oz / 100g slab bacon, diced
12 oz / 350g boneless pork butt or shoulder,
   cut into ¾-inch / 2cm cubes
6 cups / 400g shredded green cabbage
½ tsp caraway seeds
Kosher salt
Vegetable oil for frying
2 medium white onions, diced
1 large sweet red apple, peeled and shredded
1 lb / 500g sauerkraut, drained and coarsely
   chopped, plus ½ cup / 120ml brine (optional)
10 black peppercorns
3 juniper berries
2 allspice berries
2 bay leaves
1 tsp dried savory
3 Tbsp plum vodka or Redanian Herbal
   Vodka (page 247; optional)
5 oz / 150g smoked kielbasa, cubed
Sourdough bread for serving

Rinse the mushroom slices with cold water, transfer to a small bowl, cover with lukewarm water, and let soak for 1 hour.

In a separate bowl, cover the plums with lukewarm water and set aside for 30 minutes. Bring a kettle of water to a boil.

In a large nonstick skillet over medium heat, combine the bacon and a splash of cold water. Cook, stirring occasionally, until the water evaporates, 2 to 3 minutes, and continue to cook, still stirring occasionally, until the bacon is slightly browned, 4 to 5 minutes more. Add the pork cubes, turn the heat to high, and cook until browned on each side, a few minutes more. Using a slotted spoon, transfer the meat to a bowl and set the skillet aside.

Using a slotted spoon, transfer the mushrooms from their soaking liquid into a large, heavy stockpot.

Recipe continues

Line a fine-mesh sieve with a paper towel, set over the stockpot, and then pour in the soaking liquid to strain out any sediment. Set the pot over medium heat, add the cabbage, and cover with boiling water. Then add the caraway seeds and 1 tsp salt, cover, and let simmer for 30 minutes.

Meanwhile, add 2 Tbsp vegetable oil to the skillet. Set over medium heat, add the onion, and cook, stirring occasionally, until slightly browned, about 5 minutes. Add the apple and cook, stirring frequently, until slightly softened, about 5 minutes more. Transfer the contents of the skillet to the pot with the cabbage; reserve the skillet. Add the fried meat, sauerkraut, peppercorns, juniper berries, allspice berries, bay leaves, and savory to the stockpot. Stir to combine, cover, and let simmer, stirring occasionally.

After 1 hour, add the plums and their soaking water and the vodka (if using) to the stockpot and continue to simmer, uncovered, stirring occasionally until the stew reaches the desired consistency, about 1 hour. Add a splash of water if needed.

Set the skillet over medium heat, add the kielbasa, and cook, stirring occasionally, until browned, for 3 minutes. Then add to the stew, stir to combine, and let simmer for 30 minutes more. At the very end of cooking, taste the stew; if it is not sour enough, add the sauerkraut brine and season with more salt.

Serve steaming hot with chunks of sourdough bread.

NOTE: Refrigerate leftovers and reheat to enhance the flavor—transfer to a skillet and simmer, covered, for 30 minutes over medium heat once each day for two days.

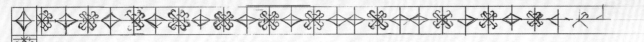

Fried Kaszanka with Egg

One morning I awoke so late as to be the sole guest in the inn's dining room. I decided to order a local specialty customarily served during the *Belleteyn* festive season. Blood sausage fried with onions and mushrooms, then topped with an egg—this was my hearty breakfast! As I ate my meal in silence I grew more and more aware. I gazed out the windows at village folk milling about. I could sense their excitement as they tended to their homesteads, preparing for the spring celebration. In keeping with local custom, they were adorning their homes with green branches while their children crowned the village cows with flower wreaths. I noted how the "young'uns" rollicked freely about the village and meadows. A local belief holds that they are watched over by a cornflower wraith—a field creature who guards the little flower hunters and makes sure they don't stray into crop rows.

⟶ MAKES 2 SERVINGS ⟶

½ oz / 15g dried mushroom slices
   (such as bay bolete or porcini)
1 Tbsp vegetable oil
1 small white onion, thinly sliced
2 tsp unsalted butter
Kosher salt
12 oz / 340g kaszanka sausage or other Polish
   black pudding, casings removed, chopped
½ tsp dried marjoram
2 eggs
Freshly ground black pepper
Sliced sourdough bread for serving

⸺ ◇ ⸺

Rinse the mushroom slices with cold water, transfer to a small bowl, cover with lukewarm water, and let soak for 1 hour. Add the mushrooms and their soaking liquid to a small saucepan and simmer until tender, about 30 minutes. Then strain the mushrooms, reserving the cooking water, and coarsely chop the mushrooms.

In a large nonstick skillet over medium heat, warm the vegetable oil. Add the onion and cook, stirring occasionally, until lightly browned, about 5 minutes. Transfer to a bowl and set aside.

In the same skillet, add the drained mushrooms and 5 Tbsp of their cooking water, turn the heat to medium, and let simmer, stirring occasionally, until the water evaporates, about 3 minutes. Add 1 tsp of the butter, season with salt, and cook, stirring occasionally, until lightly browned, 2 to 3 minutes more. Transfer to the bowl with the onion and set aside.

Add the sausage to the same skillet over medium heat, gently break up the chunks with a wooden spatula, and then add the marjoram and cook, stirring frequently, until intensely dark, 5 to 7 minutes. Then add the onion and mushrooms, season with salt and pepper, and fry, stirring thoroughly to evenly distribute the ingredients, about 3 minutes more. Divide between two serving plates, cover, and set aside.

In the same skillet over medium heat, melt the remaining 1 tsp butter and crack in the eggs. Fry until the whites are set, about 2 minutes, and then season with salt and pepper, turn the heat to low, cover, and let simmer until the yolks are partially set, 1 to 2 minutes more. Transfer an egg to each plate of fried kaszanka.

Serve immediately with slices of sourdough on the side.

Granny's Caramel-Nut Baked Apples

I have tried many varieties of apples and enjoyed quite a few, but those I tasted in White Orchard proved a rare delight. Slightly sour, filled with nuts and dried fruit, baked and topped with velvety caramel—this unexpected treat was my reward for helping a local orchardist. She was an elderly woman who needed a hand unpacking baskets in her cellar while her relatives were away. Having grown up hearing tales of old hags offering apples to naïve young girls, I accepted the baked gift with some trepidation. Luckily, despite my childish fears, the first bite brought neither misfortune nor disappointment. I sat in her kitchen, its walls adorned with pots and pans, and listened as she shared her secrets for preparing the perfect baked apple. The over-large oven in the corner, however, did make me wonder if this kind-hearted granny's dessert was not merely meant to fatten me up.

⟶ MAKES 4 SERVINGS ⟶

CARAMEL SAUCE

¼ cup / 50g granulated sugar

¼ cup / 60ml heavy cream, or as needed, at room temperature

2 Tbsp floral honey

2 pinches Zerrikanian Spice Blend (recipe follows) or ground cinnamon

1 pinch kosher salt

1 Tbsp vodka, rum, or mead, or as needed (optional)

—

1 oz / 30g mixed nuts (such as walnuts and hazelnuts), coarsely chopped

⅓ cup / 30g chopped dried cranberries

3 dried apricots, diced

2 dried plums (pitted prunes), diced

4 tart apples (such as Granny Smith)

Lemon juice for brushing

1 Tbsp unsalted butter, at room temperature

TO MAKE THE SAUCE: In a small saucepan over medium heat, melt the sugar. Shake the pan to evenly dissolve the sugar, then turn the heat to low and continue to cook until the caramel is intensely amber, about 5 minutes. Add the cream and stir vigorously; sugar lumps may form at this point, but they should completely dissolve in the cooking process. Let the sauce simmer, stirring occasionally, until smooth and resembling liquid honey, 15 to 20 minutes. Turn off the heat and let the sauce cool slightly for 10 minutes. Add the honey, spice blend, salt, and vodka (if using) and stir to incorporate. Let cool to room temperature. If the sauce becomes too thick, stir in additional cream or vodka.

In a medium bowl, combine the nuts, cranberries, apricots, plums, and 2 Tbsp of the caramel sauce. Set aside.

Recipe continues

Using a sharp knife, cut off the top ¾ inch / 2cm of each apple, so the stem is still attached. Using a small knife or a teaspoon, carve out a medium hole in the flesh to get rid of the seeds and core. Be careful not to break through the apple. Brush the inside flesh with lemon juice to prevent browning.

Preheat the oven to 350°F / 170°C.

Fill the cored apples with the caramel-nut mixture and then even out the surface of the filling by pressing gently with a spoon bottom. Cover the stuffed apples with their tops; try to match them exactly to the cutting line. Using your fingers, coat each apple with a thin layer of the butter. Transfer the apples to a baking dish.

Bake the apples, uncovered, until their skin is slightly wrinkled, 30 to 40 minutes, depending on the size and ripeness of the fruit.

Serve the apples immediately, topped with a generous portion of the remaining caramel sauce.

ZERRIKANIAN SPICE BLEND
Makes about 2 Tbsp

1 Tbsp ground cinnamon
1½ tsp ground cloves
1 tsp ground ginger
2 pinches ground nutmeg (optional)
1 pinch freshly ground black pepper (optional)
1 pinch ground cardamom (optional)
1 pinch ground allspice (optional)

In a small bowl, combine all the spices and, using a fork, mix well.

Transfer to an airtight container and store in a cool, dry place for up to 1 month.

Mahakaman Zalewajka

Everyone knows the best *zalewajka* (sour soup) is served in the dwarven homeland of Mahakam, though White Orchard's villagers claim their own to be just as good or better. There could be some truth to this given that it's a locally cherished delicacy, even among those who typically enjoy complaining—dwarven clientele included. In Mahakam, as dwarven tradition dictates, the soup is served with no cream, yet beyond the region generous dollops are added to satisfy the human palate. In the thick, sourdough broth fragrant with smoked meat and marjoram, one usually finds a variety of ingredients—mushrooms, velvety potato chunks, strips of fried onion, thick bacon bits, even slices of smoked sausage. While gathering information on this soup, I also received a piece of dwarven advice the inn's human cook, Klara, once received and took to heart: "Tradition deserves respect, sweetheart, but outside Mahakam experiment as you please . . . hungry diners will always eat!"

MAKES 4 SERVINGS

SOUP SOURDOUGH

⅓ cup / 35g dark rye flour

2 cups / 480ml boiled water, cooled to lukewarm

2 garlic cloves, lightly crushed

5 black peppercorns

2 allspice berries

2 bay leaves

Crust from 1 slice rye sourdough (optional)

—

5 oz / 150g slab bacon, diced

2 medium white onions, sliced

3 garlic cloves, chopped

7 oz / 200g chanterelle mushrooms (see Note)

Kosher salt

1 Tbsp unsalted butter

500g potatoes, peeled and cubed

2 tsp dried marjoram

3 cups / 720ml hot water

1 cup / 245g soup sourdough

Freshly ground black pepper

¼ cup / 60ml sour cream (optional)

Fresh bread for serving

TO MAKE THE SOUP SOURDOUGH: In a sterile jar, using a perfectly clean wooden spoon, stir together the rye flour and lukewarm water. Add the garlic, peppercorns, allspice berries, bay leaves, and sourdough crust (if used; it will speed up the fermentation) and stir to incorporate. Loosely cover with a clean kitchen towel. Set aside in a dark place at room temperature for 24 hours. Then, using a perfectly clean wooden spoon, stir, cover, and set aside for another day. Repeat the mixing process every 24 hours for the next 5 days. The mixture should start to smell and taste sour after about 6 days; if so, it's ready to use.

In a medium nonstick skillet over medium heat, combine the bacon and a splash of cold water. Cook, stirring occasionally, until the water evaporates, 2 to 3 minutes, and then cook until the fat melts and the bacon is lightly browned, 4 to 5 minutes more. Add the onion and continue to cook, stirring occasionally, until the onion browns, about 5 minutes. Add the garlic and stir-fry for 30 seconds, and then transfer everything to a large pot.

Recipe continues

Meanwhile, use a brush to clean any sand or dirt from the chanterelles, then transfer to a bowl, add 1 teaspoon salt, and cover with boiling water. Stir and let sit for 1 minute. Then use a slotted spoon to remove the mushrooms, discarding the soaking water. Pat mushrooms dry with a paper towel and cut larger ones, if needed, so all mushroom pieces are of similar size.

In the same skillet over medium-high heat, melt the butter. Add the chanterelles and cook, stirring only once, until lightly browned, 2 to 3 minutes. Season with salt, and then add to the pot with the bacon. Add a few tablespoons of water to the skillet and deglaze, scraping up the browned bits with a wooden spoon. Transfer the liquid to the pot.

Put the pot on the stove. Add the potatoes, marjoram, 1 tsp salt, and the hot water and bring to a boil. Then turn the heat to low, cover, and let simmer for 15 minutes until the potatoes are tender.

Using a slotted spoon, remove and discard the spices and crust (if used) from the soup sourdough and stir a few times. Slowly pour it into the pot while stirring the soup with a wooden spoon. Let the soup simmer for 15 minutes more and then season with salt and pepper.

You can also add more soup sourdough if the soup is not sour enough. If so, let simmer for a few minutes more. If the soup is too thick, add more water. Discard any unused soup sourdough after 1 week.

At the end of cooking, in a small bowl, combine ¼ cup / 60ml of the hot soup with the sour cream (if using), stir to incorporate, and then slowly pour this mixture into the pot, stirring with the wooden spoon (to prevent curdling). Turn off the heat and set aside for 2 minutes.

Serve the soup hot with hunks of fresh bread.

NOTE: If you can't buy fresh chanterelles from a local merchant, you can use an equal weight of sautéed chopped button or oyster mushrooms or a handful of dried mushroom slices (soak in lukewarm water for 40 minutes, drain, and add to the pot with the potatoes).

Campfire-Style Baked Potatoes

Before I could bid the village and innkeeper Klara a fond farewell, there was one last recipe I wished to add to my journal. As soon as the setting sun gave way to the moon's cool glow, bonfires sprang up in the meadow of a dormant orchard nearby, luring the slowly gathering inhabitants with their warmth. The sound of crackling wood and chirping grasshoppers filled the night, while the flames illuminated the bottom of a large wicker basket that concealed part of the evening's treat—herbed cottage cheese. Potatoes were dug out from amidst the hot embers at the bonfires' edges. Their soft, steaming flesh paired perfectly with the cheese—a simple snack that made the evening all the more pleasant. Bellies full, the village folk lingered by the fires until their fading glow made it clear it was time to turn in. Before heading back to the inn, I glanced one last time toward the pitch-black wall of the forest and swore I glimpsed a figure in a red cloak at its edge, abruptly vanishing into the darkness 'neath the trees.

———— ⟶ MAKES 4 SERVINGS ⟶ ————

TVOROG SPREAD
14 oz / 400g Eskel's Tvorog (page 239)
½ cup / 120ml sour cream, or as needed
5 medium radishes, diced
5 sprigs dill, chopped
5 chive stalks, chopped
1 tsp dried wild garlic (optional)
Kosher salt and freshly ground black pepper

—

5 small to medium potatoes, unpeeled
Kosher salt
¼ cup / 35g all-purpose flour
Cold-pressed flaxseed or sunflower oil for drizzling
Freshly ground black pepper
Chopped dill for garnishing

———— ⬦ ————

TO MAKE THE SPREAD: In a medium bowl, using a fork, mash the tvorog. Then add the sour cream, radishes, dill, chives, wild garlic (if using), salt and pepper and stir until combined, smooth, and thick. Add more sour cream if the spread is too crumbly. Cover and transfer to the refrigerator.

Wash the potatoes thoroughly under running water. Fill a medium pot with water, set over high heat, and bring to a boil. Add the potatoes and 1 tsp salt, cook for 5 minutes, and then drain and set aside for 1 minute to let the potatoes steam a bit.

Preheat the oven to 400°F / 200°C. In a medium bowl, combine the flour and 2 Tbsp salt. Moisten the potatoes with a little water so the coating will stick to the skin and then coat thoroughly in the flour-salt mixture. Transfer the potatoes to a baking sheet, arranging them about 2 inches / 5cm apart.

Bake the potatoes until soft (puncture with a fork to check), 40 minutes to an hour depending on size.

Transfer the baked potatoes onto serving plates. Slice each potato in half without cutting all the way through, add a generous portion of the chilled topping to the incision, drizzle with flaxseed oil, season with salt and pepper, and garnish with the dill.

NOTE: The innkeeper taught me her method for using the oven to re-create the flavors and textures of crispy potatoes baked near a campfire.

VELEN

Emerging from a literal maze of paths and shallow levees, I found myself standing at a crossroads—the first sign that I had reached Velen. In this land, wooden chapels line the roads, guiding travelers along their way like eerie will-o'-the-wisps. Guarded by the old oak Rarog, king of the local forest, the crossing reeked of damp that had wafted in from the region's mist-shrouded swamps. Unsurprisingly, local superstition holds this scrap of land to be teeming with mysterious netherworldly forces. But for some wayfarers, a different face of Velen peers through the haze of dust churned up by horses' hooves: one speckled with wooden cottages, tidy pastures and fields cultivated by generations of persistent farmers. Over time, villages in the region began to exchange goods and wares in a show of neighborly support, much to the benefit of Velen's simple cuisine. Once limited in terms of ingredients, dishes throughout the region soon evolved, while ever retaining enough unique rustic flavor to invigorate and delight any city-dweller's palate. And though Velen has for years battled vile gossip and blows to a reputation now darker than the devil himself, it is worth putting such whispered tales aside to stop at the Inn at the Crossroads, or to dine at a local family's table, so as to experience the region's warm hospitality.

Midcopse Ealdorman's Chicken Soup

with Egg Noodles

Folk wisdom cautions us to hope for the best yet be ever ready for the worst—which in my case proved to be the fickle and changeable weather I encountered in Midcopse. A sudden downpour drove me to the local ealdorman's door. The kind-hearted host and his wife invited me to stay for a meal. As regional custom would have it, "Guests in the house are gods in the house." Their humble dwelling stood fragrant with resinous wood, dust, and a savory golden decoction bubbling enticingly on the whitewashed stove. The cottage's wooden shutters and beams groaned softly as the wet weather outside heightened my desire for a few sips of what I hoped would prove a delicious, warming soup. As it turned out, the hearty broth of meat, vegetables, and herbs owed its flavor to the vegetables being roasted and to a splash of vinegar. Served with a generous helping of tender noodles made by the ealdorman's wife, the soup's aroma whisked me back to my grandmother's cozy homestead, a memory I will forever hold dear.

MAKES 4 TO 6 SERVINGS

2¼ lb / 1kg bone-in, skin-on chicken parts
   (such as thighs, drumsticks, or leg quarters)
1 lb / 450g bone-in beef (such as neck or shin)
1 bay leaf
2 allspice berries
1 tsp black peppercorns
1 Tbsp distilled white vinegar
3 medium parsley roots or parsnips, halved
2 medium carrots, halved
1 small celery root, peeled and quartered
1 large leek, white and green parts,
   trimmed and halved
1 large onion, unpeeled and halved
10 sprigs flat-leaf parsley
5 sprigs lovage
Kosher salt

EGG NOODLES
4 eggs
1 cup / 140g all-purpose flour, or as needed
Kosher salt
–
Fresh flat-leaf parsley and lovage for garnishing

Place the chicken and beef in a large pot over low heat, add cold water to cover by 2½ inches / 6½cm, and bring to a simmer. Using a slotted spoon, skim and discard any accumulated foam from the surface. Add the bay leaf, allspice berries, and peppercorns and let simmer gently, uncovered, for 1 hour. Then add the vinegar, stir, and let simmer for 1 hour more.

Recipe continues

Preheat the oven to 400°F / 200°C.

While the meat is simmering, arrange the parsley roots, carrots, celery root, leek, and onion on a baking sheet and roast until browned on the edges, 35 to 45 minutes.

Add the roasted vegetables, parsley, and lovage to the pot and continue simmering for another hour. About 15 minutes before the end of cooking, season with salt.

Set a colander or large sieve over another pot. Ladle the soup into the colander to divide the stock from the rest of the ingredients. Taste and season the stock with additional salt if needed. When the meat is cool to the touch, peel the meat from the bones, cover, and set aside. Discard the bones, skins, bay leaf, allspice berries, peppercorns, onion, leek, and herb sprigs. Cut the cooked parsley roots, carrots, and celery root into smaller chunks, cover, and set aside. (At this point, you can store the stock and solids separately in airtight containers in the fridge for up to 3 days. Reheat gently before serving.)

TO MAKE THE EGG NOODLES: In a medium bowl, whisk the eggs. Then, while continuously stirring, gradually add the flour. Season with ½ tsp salt and stir until a well-combined batter forms.

Bring a large saucepan half full of water to a boil over high heat and add 1 tsp salt. Turn the heat to medium and test the batter by gently pouring a small amount into the pot; if the dough doesn't hold together well while cooking, add more flour. Carefully pour half of the batter into the pot in a constant, thin stream, starting at the edges to create long strips of noodles. Gently stir and let simmer for 2 minutes until al dente. Drain the cooked noodles and rinse with cold water. Repeat with the remaining batter.

Pour the hot stock into individual bowls, add a few chunks of cooked vegetables, a portion of noodles, and some meat, and then garnish with chopped parsley and lovage. Serve immediately.

Sauerkraut and Split Pea Stew

Folk tales of birds abound in the North, and Velen proved no exception. Storks nesting on rooftops or swallows building dwellings within homestead walls are not pests, but marks of good fortune. A sharp eye, however, will note that alongside such lucky omens many buildings bear the scars of raids and wars. Yet these less peaceful and less prosperous times gave rise to some beloved local recipes as well. Their hand forced by circumstance, resourceful locals from Lindenvale and nearby villages nonetheless concocted filling dishes using only the simplest ingredients. For example, this sauerkraut and pea stew. Customarily boiled in a large cauldron, the rich stew is meant to last for days. It is oft served with dumplings or bread, while in happier, more abundant years it is enriched with bacon. In Velen, in these times, one might find a small, scrumptious portion left out in a clay pot for household sprites— kind imps that, in exchange for food and shelter, come nightfall help with daily chores.

MAKES 4 SERVINGS

1 cup / 200g dried yellow split peas
3 cups / 720ml boiling water
2 pinches caraway seeds
Kosher salt
5 oz / 150g slab bacon, cubed
3 Tbsp cold water, plus 1 cup / 240ml water
1 large white onion, diced
1 garlic clove, minced
1¼ lb / 570g sauerkraut, drained and coarsely chopped
1 small carrot, peeled and grated
1 tsp dried marjoram
1 bay leaf
1 allspice berry
Freshly ground black pepper

In a medium pot, rinse the split peas a few times, refreshing the water until it is clear. Then add water to cover by 2 inches / 5cm and soak at room temperature for 8 hours. Pour out the water, and replace with the boiling water, and then add the caraway seeds.

Set the pot over high heat and bring to a boil. Turn the heat to low and cook until the peas are just tender, about 15 minutes, then stir in ½ tsp salt and cook for 5 minutes more. Drain and set aside.

In a large nonstick skillet over medium heat, combine the bacon and 3 Tbsp water. Cook, stirring occasionally, about 7 to 8 minutes, until the water has evaporated, the fat melts, and the bacon is lightly browned. Add the onion and cook for 5 minutes, stirring a few times, then add the garlic and stir-fry for 30 seconds more. Set aside.

In a large pot or a 5-qt / 5L Dutch oven over high heat, combine the sauerkraut, carrot, marjoram, bay leaf, allspice berry, and remaining 1 cup / 240ml water. Cover and bring to a boil. Then turn the heat to low and let simmer, stirring occasionally, until soft, about 20 minutes.

Add the bacon-onion mixture and cooked peas to the pot. Stir vigorously, then cover and continue to simmer for 20 minutes, stirring occasionally. Remove the lid and let simmer for 5 minutes more, until most of the liquid has cooked off. Season with pepper and add more salt if needed. Serve the stew hot.

Leftover Potato Bread

Readying myself for the journey onward and with nary a clue where my next stop would be, I resolved to gather provisions for the road. Thus, a few loaves of local, freshly baked bread found their way into my saddlebags. A specialty from the village of Blackbough, this bread owes its singular flavor to the addition of beer, fried onion and—perhaps surprisingly—leftover mashed potatoes. One bite of the filling, aromatic loaf vanquished any initial doubts I may have had regarding the unusual combination. Velenese villagers also believe carrying a loaf while traveling wards off evil and brings fortuitous luck. I must admit the bread did indeed bring me good fortune once I had resumed my journey. Two nights after my departure, my horse's sensitive ears and sudden snorting warned me that nekkers had crept near my camp. I lobbed the hearty loaf I'd been enjoying at the monsters' nether paws, giving my mount and me the time we needed to make our escape.

MAKES 2 SMALL LOAVES

3 Tbsp vegetable oil

1 medium white onion, diced

Kosher salt

1 cup / 240ml lager beer (preferably unpasteurized)
   or water

1½ tsp instant yeast, or 15g fresh yeast, crumbled

1 Tbsp floral honey

1⅓ cups / 270g mashed potatoes (see Note),
   at room temperature

3 cups / 360g whole-wheat flour, with more for sprinkling

½ tsp nigella seeds (optional)

Oat bran for sprinkling (optional)

In a small nonstick skillet over medium-high heat, warm 1 Tbsp of the vegetable oil. Add the onion and a pinch of salt and cook, stirring occasionally, until golden brown, 5 to 7 minutes. Turn off the heat and set aside to cool to room temperature.

Lightly flour a work surface.

In a large bowl, combine the beer, yeast, and honey and stir just until the yeast is dissolved. Add the potatoes, flour, and 1 tsp salt. Stir until incorporated and then transfer the dough to the prepared work surface and knead for about 5 minutes. As you knead, sprinkle the dough with a little flour if needed; it should become smooth in the process but will still be quite sticky and moist. Form the dough into a ball, sprinkle with flour, and return to the bowl. Cover with a kitchen towel and leave in a warm place until the dough has doubled in size, about 1½ hours.

Line a baking sheet or a baking dish with parchment paper and lightly sprinkle with flour.

Add the remaining 2 Tbsp vegetable oil to the dough and knead for 1 to 2 minutes, then add the fried onion and knead until fully incorporated. Sprinkle the dough with flour and form into two small, narrow loaves. Place the loaves on the prepared baking sheet, sprinkle with flour, cover with the kitchen towel, and set aside at room temperature until it has almost doubled in size, about 50 minutes.

Preheat the oven to 425°F / 220°C.

When ready to bake, remove the kitchen towel and gently brush the surface of the loaves with a little water and sprinkle with the nigella seeds and oat bran (if using). Bake the loaves for 15 minutes, and then lower the oven temperature to 400°F / 200°C. Continue baking until the loaves have a dark brown crust, about 30 minutes. Turn off the oven, prop open the door, and let the bread sit in the oven for 5 minutes. Then transfer the bread to a wire rack and let cool for about 1½ hours before slicing.

The bread will stay fresh, covered, at room temperature, for up to 3 days.

NOTE: If you don't have leftover mashed potatoes, you can peel 2 medium potatoes, place them in a saucepan, and cover with water. Add 1 tsp salt and cook over medium heat until tender, about 30 minutes. Drain the potatoes, let sit for 5 minutes, and then mash. Set aside to cool to room temperature and then use for the dough.

Inn at the Crossroads' Apple and Roasted Grain Ale

When I reached the Inn at the Crossroads, I found it awash in the red glow of the setting sun. Naturally, I longed for something cold to refresh my parched throat after a full day in the saddle. As luck would have it, the inn offered a lovely bittersweet drink made of pale lager, apple juice, and a splash of roasted grain infusion. The inn's specialty, the drink was originally concocted to distinguish the establishment's fare from the watered-down beer typically served at neighboring taverns. There are times, however, when an inn's prosperity depends not on the variety of victuals on its menu, but on more unusual stratagems. In the case of the Crossroads 'twas a lucky charm fashioned from a piece of a hanged man's rope! The rumor was that the innkeep's relatives would dip the rope into the roasted grain infusion, believing that whosoever tasted a drink thus "seasoned" would be certain to return for another round. Despite my reservations about this practice and doubts as to its efficacy, fatigue, and thirst drove me to follow the other guests in draining my tankard to the last satisfying drop.

◄ MAKES 2 SERVINGS ►

¼ cup / 60ml hot water
2 tsp instant roasted barley coffee or instant chicory coffee
1 cup / 240ml pale lager, cold
1 cup / 240ml pasteurized apple juice, cold

NOTE: If you can't find instant roasted barley coffee or instant chicory coffee, you can use regular decaffeinated instant coffee.

In a small saucepan over high heat, bring the water to a boil. Remove from the heat and stir in the instant grain coffee, then set aside to cool for 5 minutes.

Add the lager and apple juice to the saucepan with the grain coffee and stir to combine.

Pour the ale into two mugs and serve immediately.

Sorcerer's Beef Stew
with Zerrikanian Spices

For years, the inconspicuous hut just beyond the village of Midcopse has served as home for a succession of herbalists. Each occupant, when moving into the cottage and inheriting the items and supplies previous tenants had left behind, assumed the role of "hedge witch," who local folk could turn to with their troubles. At the time of my visit, the hut's occupant was Yagna, who had a black rooster as her companion and clearly no patience as a cook. While ferreting through items left behind by a sorceress predecessor of hers (some signed by "Keira M." in an elegant hand), Yagna had discovered a recipe for an exquisite beef stew. Yet her hungry ambition to sample the recipe's promised fusion of dry Zurbarràn wine and Zerrikanian spices seemed doomed to go unsatisfied, so chaotic were her attempts at it. Until our chance meeting, that is. I never travel without a collection of critical provisions and have never seen any reason not to share my knowledge. So I imparted a few kitchen tips and shared several sachets straight from the Zerrikanian Spice Company in Novigrad, and soon I had turned from Yagna's unannounced guest into her culinary savior. So the right ingredients and patience enough to follow a recipe are all one needs to work culinary magic—no spells or hexes required, Madame Keira M.!

>———————◄ MAKES 4 SERVINGS ►———————

CINNAMON-CLOVE MARINADE
6 whole cloves
1 cinnamon stick
1½ cups / 360ml dry red wine
2 garlic cloves, gently crushed

—

1¼ lb / 570g boneless beef chuck
2 oz / 60g dried apricots, halved
3 Tbsp lard or neutral frying oil
2 medium red onions, thinly sliced
1 carrot, peeled, halved, and thinly sliced
Kosher salt and freshly ground black pepper
Red wine, beef stock, or water as needed
2 Tbsp floral honey
Several sprigs flat-leaf parsley, chopped
2 tsp sliced almonds, chopped
Rustic-style bread for serving

TO MAKE THE MARINADE: Place the cloves and cinnamon stick in a piece of cheesecloth and tie into a bundle.

In a medium bowl, combine the red wine, garlic, and spice bundle. Set aside.

Trim and discard any remaining fat chunks from the beef. Cut the meat against the grain into 1¼-inch / 3cm cubes, then place in the marinade and stir to coat. Cover the bowl and put in the refrigerator for at least 16 (or up to 24) hours, stirring twice during the process. About 30 minutes before cooking, remove the meat from the fridge and let sit on the counter to take the chill off.

In a small bowl, combine the dried apricots and luke-warm water to cover and let soak for 40 minutes. Drain and set aside.

Recipe continues

In a large nonstick skillet over medium-high heat, melt 1½ Tbsp of the lard. Add the onion and a pinch of salt and cook, stirring occasionally, until browned, 5 to 7 minutes. Transfer to a medium stockpot.

Remove the meat from the marinade, pat dry with paper towels, and sprinkle with salt. Transfer the remaining marinade, with the spice bundle, into the pot with the onion. Set the pot over medium heat and bring to a simmer.

In the same skillet, over high heat, melt the remaining 1½ Tbsp lard. Add half of the marinated meat, arranging the chunks to avoid crowding. Cook until the meat is browned, 1 minute on each side; do not stir; just flip the chunks on each side to brown evenly. Transfer the meat to the pot and repeat to cook the remaining meat.

Set the stockpot over low heat, cover, and bring to a simmer, stirring occasionally. After about 1½ hours, when the meat is just tender, discard the spice bundle, add the apricots and carrot, and season with salt and pepper. If most of the liquid evaporates in the process, add a splash of red wine. Continue to simmer until the stew is thick and the meat is completely soft, 30 to 45 minutes more. Turn off the heat and stir in the honey.

Serve the stew garnished with parsley and chopped almonds, along with rustic bread on the side.

Crow's Perch Game Stew
with Vodka

With its tall brick keep that towers over the countryside, Crow's Perch stands to enchant travelers to Velen even at a distance. On approaching closer, wayfarers find a small settlement at the castle's foot. Among the huts stands a simple, recently erected inn. Though opened not long ago, the inn is famed for its herbal vodka, an essential ingredient of the innkeeper's special stew, at one time, the favored meal of the local ruler, the Bloody Baron. This rich venison stew with forest mushrooms and cream marries the keep's hunting traditions with the penchant many locals have for homebrewing hooch. But everything in moderation!—as one of the drunken regulars deafeningly warned his fellow patrons, myself included. For the area around Crow's Perch is said to be teeming with imps, fiends, and fae creatures known to befuddle honest folk making their way home after an evening's liquor-fueled carousing. So, naturally, it remained unclear if the drunken regular owed his ragged clothes and empty purse to his attachment to strong drink or to invisible, mischievous beings crouched just underfoot.

— MAKES 2 TO 4 SERVINGS —

HERB AND VINEGAR MARINADE
2 cups / 480ml water
3 Tbsp apple cider vinegar
2 Tbsp floral honey
1 tsp kosher salt
1 tsp yellow mustard seeds
3 juniper berries, lightly crushed
1 allspice berry
1 bay leaf
2 pinches dried rosemary or 1 sprig rosemary
—
1 lb / 450g venison haunch or boneless beef leg
2 Tbsp all-purpose flour
2 Tbsp lard or unsalted butter
4 Tbsp / 60ml Redanian Herbal Vodka (page 247)
2 cups / 480ml vegetable stock or water, or as needed
2 juniper berries
1 bay leaf
2 pinches dried rosemary
1 oz / 30g dried mushroom slices
  (such as bay bolete or porcini)

1 Tbsp unsalted butter
1 medium onion, sliced
2 garlic cloves, minced
7 Tbsp / 100ml whipping cream
Leaves from several sprigs flat-leaf parsley,
  chopped, with more for garnishing
Kosher salt and freshly ground black pepper
Sourdough bread for serving

—◇—

TO MAKE THE MARINADE: In a medium bowl, combine the water, vinegar, honey, salt, mustard seeds, juniper berries, allspice berry, bay leaf, and rosemary and stir to incorporate. Set aside.

Trim and discard any connective tissue from the venison. Cut the meat against the grain into 1¼-inch / 3cm cubes and transfer to the bowl with the marinade.

Recipe continues

Cover and put in the refrigerator for 24 hours, stirring twice during the process. About 1 hour before cooking, remove the meat from the fridge, drain and discard the marinade, and let sit on the counter to take the chill off. Pat the meat dry with paper towels.

In a small bowl, combine the flour and meat. Toss to coat and then shake off the excess flour.

In a large nonstick skillet over medium-high heat, melt the lard. Add the marinated meat, arranging the chunks so as not to crowd the pan. Cook until the meat is browned, about 1 minute on each side; do not stir; just flip the chunks on each side to brown evenly. Add the vodka, shake the pan, and cook for 2 to 3 minutes, until the liquid evaporates.

Transfer the meat to a medium stockpot over low heat. Add the vegetable stock, juniper berries, bay leaf, and rosemary, then cover and let simmer for 1 hour.

Meanwhile, rinse the mushrooms with cold water, place in a small bowl, cover with lukewarm water, and let soak for 40 minutes. Strain and reserve the soaking water.

In the same skillet over low heat, melt the butter. Add the onion and cook, stirring occasionally, until lightly browned, about 4 minutes. Add the drained mushrooms and cook until lightly browned, about 5 minutes more. Then add the garlic and stir-fry for 30 seconds. Add ¾ cup / 180ml of the mushroom soaking water, stirring to scrape up any browned bits with a wooden spoon. Turn the heat to high and cook until almost all the water evaporates. Transfer the contents of the skillet to the stockpot. Continue to simmer the stew, uncovered, and stirring often, until the meat and mushrooms are completely soft, about 1 hour more. Discard the bay leaf and juniper berries.

Slowly pour the whipping cream into the stew, while stirring with the wooden spoon. Add the chopped parsley and continue to simmer, uncovered, until the stew thickens, about 10 minutes. Season with salt and pepper, if needed. Garnish with parsley leaves.

Serve the stew immediately with chunks of sourdough bread on the side.

Aunt Lutka's Flatbread

Lake Wyndamer was still shrouded in morning fog when life began to stir around the village huts. Soon, warm flatbreads made by my hostess, Lutka, began landing on her straw plate. Lutka insisted I call her *aunt* and gladly taught me how to prepare this simplest of breads. The dough, made from but a few ingredients, is sometimes spiced up with nigella seeds or wild garlic. Once baked, the flatbreads are served with honey, jam or cottage cheese, as is one's preference. Sitting on the fishing pier with my own batch later that morning, I enjoyed my delicious snack and the lake's calm surface, deep beneath which a water nymph is said to languish, unhappily in love with a human being. Ensconced in my web of thoughts, I slowly tore off pieces of flatbread and used them to scoop honey from a small clay pot . . .

MAKES 5 FLATBREADS

¾ cup / 105g all-purpose flour
¾ cup / 90g whole-wheat flour or spelt flour, with more for sprinkling
⅔ cup / 160ml hot water, or as needed
1 tsp kosher salt
1 tsp spices/herbs (such as nigella seeds, wild garlic, or dried thyme; optional)
Honey or plum jam for serving

In a medium bowl, using a fork, combine both flours, the hot water, salt, and spices/herbs (if using) into a sticky dough. Sprinkle a work surface with whole-wheat flour and then tip the dough onto the surface. Knead the dough for a few minutes, sprinkling with more whole-wheat flour or adding more water, if needed, until it becomes soft, elastic, and less sticky. Cover with a bowl and let rest for 15 minutes.

Separate the dough into five portions and form them into very thin, 5-inch / 13cm oval flatbreads, about ¹⁄₁₆ inch / 2mm thick. You can also flatten them using a rolling pin. Set aside.

Set a medium dry nonstick skillet over medium-high heat. Add two or three of the flatbreads and cook until air bubbles and dark brown spots appear on the surface, about 90 seconds on each side. Transfer to a serving plate and repeat with the remaining flatbreads.

The flatbreads are best when eaten right away, served as a side or as a stand-alone snack drizzled with honey or spread with plum jam.

Boris the Troll's Hotchpotch Zoup

A board nailed to a post, bearing the lopsided inscription "Trol's Gud Eat-Inn," hinted that Velen could be a place where I might very well expect the unexpected. A path beginning just past the post led to a clearing where someone had arranged boulders to serve as tables and benches. The "inn" belonged to a troll named Boris, while a peasant named Bolan, a partner in the enterprise, assisted in indulging his monstrous friend's culinary dreams. Their unusual troll-human partnership gave locals the necessary confidence to sample the contents of the troll's cauldron. I managed to sneak a peek inside myself. The bubbling mash seemed to contain every possible ingredient—different meats, vegetables, fried onions, and a variety of mushrooms—but it soon surprised me with its pleasant aroma and unique flavor. Zoup à la corpse, nekker stew, and elf and onion chowder remained merely catchy names from the troll's repertoire. As offered at the eatery, at Bolan's behest, certain original ingredients had been replaced with things more suitable to the human palate and stomach.

—— MAKES 8 SERVINGS ——

14 oz / 400g beef chuck
9 oz / 250g pork shoulder
3 qt / 3L cold water, or as needed
Kosher salt
2 bay leaves
2 allspice berries
2 carrots, peeled
2 parsley roots or parsnips, peeled
2 medium potatoes, peeled and cubed
1½ tsp dried savory
5 oz / 150g slab bacon, diced
7 oz / 200g smoked kielbasa, diced
5 oz / 150g sliced oyster or button mushrooms
1 oz / 30g dried wood ear or mun mushrooms, soaked in lukewarm water for 15 minutes and then drained (optional)
3 garlic cloves, chopped
2 Tbsp vegetable oil
3 medium red onions, thickly sliced

⅓ cup / 80g tomato paste
2 Tbsp all-purpose flour
¼ cup / 20g chopped fresh flat-leaf parsley
Freshly ground black pepper
Sour cream for serving

——— ◇ ———

Place the beef and pork in a large stockpot over low heat. Cover with about 2 qt / 2L of the cold water, add 1½ tsp salt, and bring to a simmer. Using a slotted spoon, skim and discard any accumulated foam from the surface. Add the bay leaves and allspice berries, cover, and let simmer gently. After 1½ hours, add the carrots and parsley roots and continue to simmer until the meat is soft, 30 to 40 minutes more. Strain, discard the bay leaves and allspice berries, and then transfer the stock back into the pot.

Recipe continues

Cut the cooked meat into small chunks, trimming away any fat or connective tissue. Cube the carrots and parsley roots. Transfer the meat, carrots, and parsley roots to the stockpot; add the potatoes, savory, 1 tsp salt, and remaining 1 qt / 1L water, as needed to cover the solids; cover; and return to a simmer.

Meanwhile, in a medium nonstick skillet over medium heat, combine the bacon and kielbasa and cook, stirring occasionally, until both are lightly browned, about 10 minutes. Then transfer to the stockpot.

In the same skillet over medium heat, using the remaining fat, combine the oyster and wood ear mushrooms (if using) and cook without stirring for 4 minutes, then stir and continue to cook for 3 minutes more. Add the garlic and stir-fry for 30 seconds. Season with salt, stir, and transfer to the stockpot.

In the same skillet over medium heat, warm the oil. Add the onion and a pinch of salt and cook, without stirring, until heavily browned, about 5 minutes. Then flip the onion, brown on the other side, about 3 minutes more, and transfer to the stockpot.

In the same skillet, over medium heat, add the tomato paste and stir-fry for 1 minute. Add a splash of the soup stock and deglaze the skillet, scraping up the browned bits with a wooden spoon. Transfer the skillet contents to the stockpot.

Let the soup simmer until the potatoes are completely soft. If there's not enough liquid to cover the potatoes, add 1 to 2 cups / 240 to 480ml water. At the end of cooking, in a small bowl, whisk the flour with a tablespoon or two of cold water and then stir into the stockpot. Season the soup with salt, if needed, and let simmer for about 5 minutes. Then add the parsley, season generously with pepper, and let simmer for 5 minutes more.

Serve the soup immediately with a dollop of sour cream.

VELEN

Forefathers' Eve Toffee Candy

Food is ever an important part of holiday celebrations, whether as lovingly prepared dishes served at family feasts or plain crops offered humbly to the gods just after harvest. It is no different during Forefathers' Eve, a rite that brings most of Fyke Isle's folk together. On the night in question, the line between the worlds of the living and dead is blurred, allowing humans to commune with the spirits of dead ancestors. Treats made of nuts, dried fruit, and honey are prepared as offerings for these souls. Among the living, meanwhile, toffee candies made from heavy whipping cream and any leftovers from the offerings have come to be so popular as to now be made and eaten year-round, be it Forefathers' Eve or not. I was thus able to sample these delicious, sticky, sweet-and-salty candies—just one of many secret treats waiting to be discovered in Velen.

---- ► MAKES 36 PIECES ► ----

1 cup / 200g granulated sugar
½ cup / 125ml heavy whipping cream, at room temperature
2 Tbsp unsalted butter
Kosher salt
1 Tbsp poppy seeds
3½ oz / 100g mixed nuts (such as hazelnuts, walnuts, and almonds)
1 Tbsp floral honey
⅓ cup / 50g diced dried fruits (such as apricots, cranberries, plums, and raisins)
Vegetable oil for brushing

Set a medium saucepan with a light-colored bottom over medium heat. Add ½ cup / 100g of the sugar and cook, shaking the pan occasionally but not stirring, until most of the sugar dissolves and turns amber. Be careful not to burn the sugar at this point; if it starts to turn dark brown, proceed immediately to the next step.

Add the cream to the pan, then turn the heat to medium-low, stir vigorously with a wooden spoon to combine, then stir in the remaining ½ cup / 100g sugar, and let simmer, stirring occasionally, until all the sugar has dissolved and the mixture is thick and a very deep amber, about 20 minutes. If clumps of sugar remain, remove them with a fork and proceed to the next step.

Add the butter and 2 pinches of salt to the saucepan, stir to combine, and continue to simmer for 5 minutes more. Drop a teaspoon of the hot caramel into a bowl of cold water, wait a moment, then use your fingers to form the caramel into a ball; it's ready to use if it holds its shape but is still a little pliable. Turn off the heat, stir in the poppy seeds and let this candy mixture cool off for 5 minutes.

Meanwhile, in a medium, dry nonstick skillet over medium heat, toast the nuts, shaking the pan a few times, until they are slightly browned, about 3 minutes. Turn off the heat, transfer the nuts to a cutting board, let them cool slightly, and then coarsely chop.

Once the candy mixture is warm, but not hot, add the honey, nuts, and dried fruits and stir thoroughly to incorporate.

Recipe continues

Line a 6-inch / 15cm square container with parchment paper and brush with vegetable oil, pour in the candy mass, and, using a spatula, spread it out evenly. Cover and let sit at room temperature for about 2 hours, then transfer to the refrigerator for 2 hours.

Remove the pan from the fridge and remove the candy block from the pan. Using a sharp knife, cut the block into 1¼-inch / 3cm cubes. Wrap each individual candy in a piece of parchment paper or wax paper.

The candy can be stored in the fridge for up to 2 weeks.

VARIATION: If you would like a less-sweet version, omit the dried fruits and replace them with an additional 1 oz / 30g of nuts.

Ladies of the Wood Gingerbread Cookies

It wouldn't be a proper Heatherton honey harvest without crunchy decorations hanging from trees and shrubs around the village. These sweet, richly decorated gingerbread cookies, baked by local housewives, vary in shape and hue depending on the spices within. Children especially love that these tempting delicacies dangle from colorful threads and ribbons, and just barely within reach of their fingertips. Yet the sweet objects of desire are said to be guarded by the sinister Ladies of the Wood, out to snare the more mischievous of the children. How did such an unusual custom arise among the inhabitants of the recently rebuilt village? And do the evil Crones of remote Crookback Bog actually snatch children wandering down the sweet-lined path? The stories surrounding this custom fade as time passes and change as they migrate to distant places. In one instance they are said to have inspired a folk tradition whereby villagers dress up in costumes fashioned from straw! Imagine! Yet, well-seasoned reader of stories that I am, I can say even the most improbable story almost always contains a grain of truth.

◄———— MAKES ABOUT 24 COOKIES ————►

3 Tbsp lard (see Note) or unsalted butter

3 Tbsp granulated sugar

3 Tbsp floral honey

2 Tbsp milk

1 egg

1⅓ cups / 160g whole-wheat flour, with more for sprinkling

2 tsp Zerrikanian Spice Blend (page 42) or store-bought sugarless gingerbread spice

½ tsp baking soda

1 pinch kosher salt

ICING

¾ cup plus 1 Tbsp / 100g confectioners' sugar, or as needed

2 Tbsp water, or as needed

2 or 3 drops lemon juice, or as needed

2 drops raspberry or cherry syrup, or as needed (optional)

—

1 handful sugar sprinkles (optional)

In a small saucepan over medium heat, combine the lard, granulated sugar, honey, and milk, stirring occasionally until it comes to a simmer. Turn off the heat and let cool until lukewarm.

Using a fork, whisk the egg into the mixture, then add the flour, spice blend, baking soda, and salt and stir thoroughly to combine. Cover and refrigerate for at least 24 hours before baking; the cookies will taste better if you let the dough remain in the fridge for a few days. Remove the dough from the fridge and let sit at room temperature for about 30 minutes to take the chill off.

Preheat the oven to 350°F / 170°C. Line a baking sheet with parchment paper.

Recipe continues

Sprinkle a work surface with flour, tip out the dough, and knead a few times. Then, using a rolling pin, roll out the dough to a ⅛ inch / 3mm thickness (the dough will slightly rise during baking). Using a cookie cutter or 2½-inch- / 6.5cm-diameter drinking glass, cut the dough into shapes. Reroll the scraps and cut out additional cookies. Arrange the cookies on the prepared baking sheet, leaving 1¼ inches / 3cm between each.

Bake the cookies until they are just slightly brown on top, 12 to 15 minutes. (They will be quite soft at this point but will firm up after cooling.) Remove the cookies from the oven, transfer to a wire rack, and let cool completely.

TO MAKE THE ICING: In a small bowl, whisk the confectioners' sugar with the water and either 2 drops of the lemon juice or 2 drops of the raspberry syrup (if you would like the icing tinted), until the mixture becomes smooth and thick. Add additional sugar if it becomes too runny or more water if it's too thick.

Brush each cookie with icing, scatter some sugar sprinkles (if using) on top, and then set aside until the icing sets.

Store the cookies at room temperature in an airtight container for up to 3 weeks.

NOTE: If you are using lard, the heated mixture may smell repelling but don't be discouraged—the cookies will taste great!

OXENFURT

With its Academy renowned throughout the North, Oxenfurt is the crown jewel of Redania. Widely considered to be a capital of entertainment in addition to higher learning, the city is a bustling haven of narrow, colorful streets teeming with students, artists, professors and travelers. Once per quarter, the city's crème de la crème welcomes an invigorating influx of guests to the auction house—eccentrics and lovers of antiques, artwork and curiosities, they come from all four corners of the world. In addition to the quarterly bidding wars at the house, the city's economy remains robust year-round thanks to skilled craftsfolk, savvy merchants and experienced owners of inns, wineries and other enterprises. Even in the off-season, these diverse firms generate lavish profits. Each morning, countless goods pass through the city's gates, transported from the river docks or the villages scattered along the opposite bank of the Pontar. Proudly displayed on color-ful market stalls, the products will become the various dishes served in city taverns or the homes of the bourgeoisie. The most popular of Oxenfurt's many inns is without a doubt the Alchemy, ever crowded with rowdy guests and city guards on prolonged breaks—all thirsting for fun and endless rounds of tankards filled to the brim. From here emerge many of the rakish souls who roam the city day and night, bellowing drinking songs.

Academy All-Nighter Brined Cucumbers

My plans took me to Oxenfurt to attend to some family business. Given the opportunity, I resolved to meet up with old friends from my time at Lan Exeter University, all now employed by Oxenfurt Academy's Faculty of Technology—or, as its students would humorously have it, the "Deus Ex Machina." My first evening in the city saw me unpack in the student lodgings, available for travelers to rent while students are away. I then set out to find the address my companions of yore had appointed for our reunion. The festivities were underway by the time I arrived, and my friends greeted me with tipsy huzzahs. Just like old times . . . we started with nip glasses of something strong and an appetizer from the house larder. My companions had prepared the favored snack of busy academics such as themselves: crunchy cucumbers brined with garlic, dill, and horseradish, as per the tried-and-true Oxenfurt Drinker's Club recipe. Our samplings of liquors, pickled tidbits and lard-smeared bread soon inspired a round of "Ne'er Have I Ever," during which I detailed my unfortunate nekker-occasioned loss of Leftover Potato Bread in Velen—to peals of laughter, I might add.

MAKES TWO 1-QUART / 1L JARS

12 pickling or Kirby cucumbers
1 qt / 1L water
2 Tbsp coarse Kosher salt without additives
6 large sprigs dill, preferably with flower heads
1 tsp yellow mustard seeds
2½-inch / 6.5cm piece horseradish root, peeled and sliced into 4 pieces
4 garlic cloves, halved

In a large bowl, combine the cucumbers with enough cold water to cover and let sit for 2 hours. Drain and wash thoroughly under running water to get rid of any sand residue, cut off the ends, then set aside.

In a large saucepan over high heat, bring the 1 qt / 1L water to a boil. Turn off the heat and let cool until the water is lukewarm, then add the salt and stir to dissolve.

Sterilize two 1-qt / 1L jars and jar lids with boiling water.

In the bottom of each jar, place 3 dill sprigs and ½ tsp of the mustard seeds. Add the cucumbers vertically, tightly packing as many as you can into the jar. Place 2 horse-radish slices and 2 garlic cloves in the remaining space between the cucumbers. Completely cover the cucumbers with the lukewarm salted water—nearly to the top of the jar. (If you need additional water, prepare another portion, as described previously.)

Recipe continues

Put the jars on a plate or tray to catch any brine that spills over during fermentation. Loosely twist on the jar lids to allow some air flow, place the jars at room temperature in a dark place, and let them sit for 4 to 5 days until the water becomes very cloudy and the cucumbers have started to turn a duller green. Then tightly close the lids, transfer to the refrigerator, and let them sit for about 1 week before serving. The longer the cucumbers sit in the brine, the more sour they will become.

Brined cucumbers can be stored in the fridge for up to 3 months.

NOTES

These will be edible in just a few days, with a crunchy green center and brined skin. At this stage they are great as a snack or for pairing with the Lard Spread (page 140). For Brined Cucumber Soup (page 115), they must be fully translucent on the inside and brined for at least 1½ weeks.

The brining liquid should be cloudy. A white film may develop on the surface; this is a normal part of fermentation. However, if you see any mold on the jar, lid, or brine, or notice a strong, unpleasant smell, discard the cucumbers and start a new batch.

Alchemy Inn's Bacon
Baked in Redanian Lager

Cursing the infuriating storm that hung over the city, I pulled up my rain-soaked hood and directed my steps to where the sound of music and song and the clinking of mugs echoes day and night . . . and where they serve an irresistible local specialty. Once across the Alchemy Inn's doorstep, I removed my dripping cloak with relief and entered the stuffy interior, more crowded than usual that day due to a dice poker tournament. I made my way through the excited throng of onlookers, exercising all my patience and determination (while adding a few elbow jabs) to reach the innkeeper. I then waited as he poured endless tankards of Redanian lager, Rivian kriek, and Kaedweni stout, shouting directly past my ear for guests to pick up their orders. But my prize for waiting so patiently was worth it: bacon baked with beer, garlic, and savory, served with a dollop of plum jam and a chunk of fresh bread.

━━━━◄ MAKES 10 SERVINGS ►━━━━

2¼ lb / 1kg boneless pork belly
1 Tbsp dried savory
1 Tbsp kosher salt
½ tsp freshly ground black pepper
2 garlic cloves, crushed and peeled
¾ cup / 175ml pale lager beer
Plum jam for serving

—————◇—————

Wash the meat under running water, and then pat it dry with paper towels.

In a small bowl, combine the savory, salt, and pepper. Rub the meat thoroughly on each side with this spice mixture. Transfer the meat to a baking dish, cover, and refrigerate for 12 to 24 hours.

About 45 minutes before baking, remove the meat from the fridge and let sit on the counter to take the chill off. Preheat the oven to 430°F / 220°C.

Roast the meat, uncovered, for 15 minutes, then lower the oven temperature to 300°F / 150°C, add the garlic, pour in the beer, cover with aluminum foil or a lid, and bake for 1½ hours more. Baste the meat with the baking juices six times during the process. Turn the oven temperature to 430°F / 220°C, uncover the dish, and roast until the top is nicely browned, about 25 minutes. Remove from the oven and let rest for 20 minutes.

Slice the meat and serve hot or cold with plum jam.

Crimson Beetroot Soup
with Cherries and Potato Purée

My sense of orientation in Oxenfurt's labyrinthine streets gradually improved. So I dared to venture forth from the area around the Philosopher's Gate in search of dinner. My destination—a square where minstrels present small puppet shows. They tell tales fantastic—of a prince from a land across the seas turned into a toad, of a Temerian princess turned into a striga, and of a shifty warlock who lived on the Moon. This attraction for the city's youngsters proved to be around the corner from a new, fashionable inn opened in an old warehouse. The warehouse had shut down due to repeated disappearances of chests, barrels, and other trade parcels. Clearly a bad omen, this failed to dissuade the new owners, who opened the Wallcreeper Inn to serve a unique menu of exclusively crimson-hued dishes. "When in REDania . . ." I chuckled to myself as I ate the beetroot soup with cherries, taking a spoonful of creamy potato purée and butter-fried onion, then submerging it in the slightly sweet crimson concoction.

— MAKES 2 TO 4 SERVINGS —

4 medium beets
1 large carrot
4 garlic cloves
3 Tbsp vegetable oil
3 tsp unsalted butter
1 large onion, diced
Kosher salt
4 cups / 960ml vegetable stock, chicken stock,
    or water, or as needed
⅓ cup / 85g fresh or frozen sour cherries,
    pitted and chopped
1 bay leaf
2 allspice berries
1 Tbsp apple cider vinegar, or as needed
4 medium russet or Yukon gold potatoes, peeled
Heaping 2 Tbsp sour cream
Freshly ground black pepper
Floral honey or granulated sugar for sweetening (optional)

Preheat the oven to 375°F / 190°C.

Rinse the beets under running water, pat dry with a paper towel, and then arrange on a baking sheet with the carrot and garlic. Drizzle 2 Tbsp of the vegetable oil over the top and toss to coat.

Roast the vegetables for about 35 minutes, and then remove the garlic. Peel and discard the skins, finely chop the garlic, and then transfer to a large stockpot. Continue roasting the vegetables until soft (stick a knife in one to check), about 1½ hours.

Meanwhile, in a medium nonstick skillet over medium-high heat, warm the remaining 1 Tbsp vegetable oil and 1 tsp of the butter. Add the onion and a pinch of salt, and cook, stirring occasionally, until golden brown, 6 to 8 minutes. Transfer two-thirds of the onion into the stockpot and set aside the remaining one-third.

Recipe continues

Remove the beets and carrot from the oven and let cool slightly, so you can peel the beets with your bare hands. Using a box grater, on the side with the largest holes, shred two of the beets and the carrot. Then on the side with the smaller holes, shred the remaining two beets. Transfer the beets and carrot to the pot.

Set the pot over low heat. Add the vegetable stock, cherries, bay leaf, allspice berries, vinegar, and 2 tsp salt. Bring to a simmer and cook gently until the vegetables are completely soft, 50 to 60 minutes.

Meanwhile, in a medium saucepan over high heat, combine the potatoes with water to cover and bring to a boil. Add 1 tsp salt, cover, and let simmer until completely soft, about 30 minutes. Drain and let sit for 2 minutes, then, using a potato masher, mash thoroughly. Add the sour cream, remaining 2 tsp butter, and reserved fried onion and stir vigorously with a wooden spoon to combine. Keep warm.

Strain the soup through a fine-mesh sieve set over a large bowl. Using a potato masher, press as much liquid as possible from the vegetables. Return the stock and half of the pressed vegetables to the pot. You can add more vegetables if you want the soup to be thicker and chunkier, or you can blend with an immersion blender to get a smoother consistency.

Season the soup with pepper and more salt, if needed. You can adjust the sweet-sour balance by adding a little honey or sugar or more vinegar.

Pour the soup into bowls and serve immediately, with the potatoes on the side.

Fried Chicken Livers with Pears

Every first Thursday of the month, at one of their Oxenfurt residences, the Vegelbud family hosts a lavish dinner for friends and carefully selected poets, scholars, artists, and craftsfolk. As luck would have it, I managed to secure an invitation to this exclusive affair. I was to represent our family firm—at the time, our Koviri workshop was crafting a special order placed by the Vegelbuds. My presence also allowed my nosy relatives to check on me from a distance, my timely arrival confirming that my journey was proceeding according to plan. But I digress. The multicourse meal began with delicate, mouthwatering chicken livers, sautéed with onion and served with caramelized pears. The exquisite composition is based on a famous recipe originated by the chef at the Cunny of the Goose Inn. After a first course of that caliber, I could only imagine the delicacies yet to be served . . .

⤛ MAKES 2 SERVINGS ⤜

7 oz / 200g chicken livers
1 cup / 240ml whole milk
1 tsp unsalted butter
2 medium pears, cut into eighths
½ cup / 120ml apple cider or semidry white wine
2 Tbsp lard or vegetable oil
1 small onion, thinly sliced
Kosher salt
1½ Tbsp all-purpose flour
½ tsp dried marjoram, with more for sprinkling
Freshly ground black pepper

Trim and discard any connective tissue and fat residue from the livers and then halve any larger livers, so each is a similar size. Transfer the livers to a small bowl, add the milk, and let soak for 1 hour at room temperature. Drain and thoroughly pat dry with paper towels.

In a large nonstick skillet over medium-high heat, melt the butter. Add the pears and cook on one side for 2 minutes, then flip and continue to cook until golden brown, 1 to 2 minutes more. Add ¼ cup / 60ml of the cider and cook until the liquid evaporates, about 2 minutes. Transfer the pears to a serving plate, cover with aluminum foil, and keep warm.

In the same skillet over medium-high heat, melt 1 Tbsp of the lard. Add the onion and a pinch of salt and cook, stirring occasionally, until soft, about 4 minutes. Move the onions to the side of the skillet to make room.

In a small bowl, combine the flour and livers and toss to coat, shaking off the excess flour. In the same skillet over medium-high heat, melt the remaining 1 Tbsp lard, then add the livers, and cook until well browned, about 3 minutes. Using tongs, flip the livers and cook until the second sides are well-browned, 2 minutes more. Add the remaining ¼ cup / 60ml cider, stir together with the onions and livers, scraping the bottom of the pan with a wooden spoon, and cook until the liquid evaporates and the livers are nicely browned on both sides, about 2 minutes more. Slice into one of the livers at the thickest part to confirm they are fully cooked through. If needed, cover with a lid and stew for 2 minutes more. Add the marjoram, season with salt and pepper, and stir to combine. Transfer the livers to the plate with the pears. Rub a pinch of marjoram between your fingers and sprinkle on top.

Serve the livers and pears immediately.

Tretogor Cabbage Rolls

As the feast at the Vegelbuds' home continued, the table was filled and refilled with dishes in the multitudes. Among them I spotted the famed Tretogorian baked cabbage rolls. A fragrant dish of browned cabbage leaves wrapped around a savory filling of barley, meat, and mushrooms, the rolls were served topped with a velvety dill cream sauce. The conversation *à table* revolved around recent scientific achievements at the Academy, art gallery openings, and paintings by old masters and rising stars alike—a topic about which the guests from the auction house were especially excited. Of course, there was no avoiding the Vegelbuds' boasting about their most recent acquisitions for their many estates. I thus heard quite a bit of praise for my family's craft. Suddenly, I was inundated with requests from the other guests wishing to take advantage of my presence! So I employed a strategy of polite yet tight-lipped answers and sought mostly to hide behind my plate . . . the better to enjoy its delectable contents.

MAKES 12 ROLLS

½ oz / 15g dried mushroom slices
   (such as bay bolete or porcini)
2 oz / 60g stale bread roll
½ cup / 100g pearl barley
1 cup / 240ml water
Kosher salt
1 Tbsp neutral vegetable oil, with more for brushing
1 onion, diced
1 tsp unsalted butter
9 oz / 250g button mushrooms, chopped
Freshly ground black pepper
One 2½-lb / 1.1kg head green cabbage,
   cored, and outer leaves discarded
1 Tbsp distilled white vinegar or apple cider vinegar
9 oz / 250g ground pork
2 tsp dried marjoram
½ cup / 120ml vegetable stock or water

DILL SAUCE
2 Tbsp unsalted butter
2 Tbsp all-purpose flour
1½ cups / 360ml whole milk, at room temperature
⅓ cup / 25g chopped fresh dill
2 Tbsp lemon juice
Kosher salt and freshly ground black pepper

Rinse the dried mushrooms under cold water, transfer to a small bowl, cover with lukewarm water, and let soak for 30 minutes. Strain the mushrooms and reserve the mushroom-soaking water. Set the mushrooms aside. Place the stale roll in the mushroom water and let soak for 10 minutes until soft, then drain and transfer to a large bowl.

Put the barley in a fine-mesh sieve, rinse under cold water, and then transfer to a medium stockpot over medium-high heat. Add the 1 cup / 240ml water and ½ tsp salt, cover, and bring to a boil. Then turn the heat to low and cook for 15 minutes. Turn off the heat, stir, cover, and then set aside until the barley is tender, about 5 minutes. The barley should soak up all the water; if it doesn't, then drain. Transfer to the bowl with the roll. Using a fork, lightly mash the barley and roll until combined.

In a large nonstick skillet over medium-high heat, warm the vegetable oil. Add the onion and a pinch of salt and cook, stirring occasionally, until golden brown, 5 to 7 minutes. Transfer to the bowl.

Recipe continues

In the same skillet, over medium heat, melt the butter. Add the button and rehydrated mushrooms and cook, without stirring, for 3 minutes. Then stir once and continue to cook until the water has evaporated and the mushrooms are lightly browned, a few minutes more. Season with salt and pepper and transfer to the bowl.

Bring a kettle of water to a boil. Place the cabbage in a large stockpot over medium-high heat, cored-side up, cover with boiling water almost to the top, and add the vinegar. Turn the heat to low and let simmer for 5 minutes. While the cabbage is simmering, use tongs to carefully pull off the first layer of leaves and set them aside on a large cutting board, then proceed to pull off the rest of the leaves. (If the remaining leaves are hard to pull off, let the cabbage simmer for a few minutes more to soften.) Trim and discard the thick ribs at the end of each leaf.

When the ingredients in the large bowl have cooled to room temperature, add the ground pork, marjoram, about 1 tsp salt, and a generous grinding of pepper. Using your hands, knead the ingredients until this filling is well incorporated and moist. If it feels too dry, add a splash of water and continue kneading.

Spoon 2 to 3 Tbsp of filling toward the base of each cabbage leaf, fold in the sides of the leaves, covering the filling, and tightly roll to enclose. Repeat with the remaining filling to form about sixteen rolls.

Preheat the oven to 350°F / 180°C.

Brush a deep baking dish with vegetable oil, line the bottom with a layer of the remaining cabbage leaves, and then arrange the cabbage rolls, seam-side down, tightly next to each other. Brush the tops with vegetable oil, pour in the vegetable stock, and cover with aluminum foil.

Bake the cabbage rolls for about 40 minutes, then uncover, turn the oven temperature to 400°F / 200°C and continue to bake until nicely browned, about 20 minutes more.

TO MAKE THE DILL SAUCE: Meanwhile, in a small saucepan over medium heat, melt the butter. Add the flour and cook, stirring vigorously with a whisk, for 1 minute. Gradually add the milk, while stirring continuously, then turn the heat to low and let simmer, stirring frequently, until thickened, for 5 minutes. Stir in the dill and lemon juice, season with salt and pepper, and cook for 2 minutes more, then turn off the heat. The sauce should have the consistency of liquid honey; if it's too runny, continue to cook until it thickens to the desired consistency.

Remove the cabbage rolls from the oven and let rest for 10 minutes, then transfer to a serving plate.

Ladle a generous portion of dill sauce on top of the cabbage rolls and serve immediately.

Confectionery Apple Fritters

A crowd had already gathered by the city gate by the time it opened at sunrise. Aedirnian merchants, eager to reach the market, had blocked the narrow street with their carts. Before I could pass, I was forced to witness them arguing with city guards and a tax collector about inconsistent treatment of their respective cargoes. By the time the matter was resolved, the market was slowly waking, the merchants busy arranging their goods in their stalls. The stands were piled high with goat cheeses, fresh fish, vegetables, and fruit. Yet I sought a confectioner's stall, hoping to get some sweet apple fritters from the morning's first batch. I found my quarry near the city well. As expected, I was not the sole early bird waiting to catch a first bite. The fluffy, warm apple fritters cupped in the palm of my hand quickly awakened my senses—a most welcome treat to calm my nerves that first day of a new assignment at the antique shop belonging to the auction house.

MAKES 12 TO 14 FRITTERS

2 eggs, separated
3 Tbsp granulated sugar
1 cup / 240ml buttermilk, at room temperature
1 cup / 140g all-purpose flour
½ cup / 60g medium rye flour
1 tsp baking soda
Kosher salt
1 medium apple, cored and shredded
Vegetable oil for frying
Confectioners' sugar for sprinkling
Ground cinnamon for sprinkling
Plum or strawberry jam for serving

In a medium bowl, combine the egg yolks and granulated sugar and, using a whisk, mix together until creamy. Then add the buttermilk and whisk until incorporated. Stir in both flours, the baking soda, and a pinch of salt. Once incorporated, add the apple and mix gently until just combined into a batter.

In a separate metal bowl, combine the egg whites and a pinch of salt and, using a whisk, whip into soft peaks.

Gently stir one-third of the whites into the batter and then, using a spatula, gently fold in the remaining two-thirds.

Line a plate with a double layer of paper towels.

In a large nonstick skillet over medium heat, warm ¼ inch / 6mm of vegetable oil until it is shimmering and a drop of flour added to the oil sizzles. Using a large spoon, scoop up 2 Tbsp portions of the batter and drop in the hot oil, flattening each with the bottom of the spoon. Take care not to crowd the pan. Fry the fritters until browned, 2 to 3 minutes on each side.

Transfer the fritters to the prepared plate to drain. Repeat with the remaining batter, adding more oil if needed.

Serve the fritters hot or at room temperature, sprinkled with confectioners' sugar and cinnamon and topped with jam.

Merchant's Cucumber Cooler

"Damn wind's howling," muttered a white-haired man looking for a dry corner near the gate, shelter to last out the storm. It was a perfect echo of my own thoughts on that awful day. Hood drawn, I leapt over puddles, managing to keep dry all the way from the antique shop to the market I visited during afternoon breaks. The stall keepers had come to expect my appearances and eagerly offered delicacies I'd never dreamt of. The list of my favorites, apple fritters ever at the top, quickly grew to include a cucumber cooler—a sweet-and-sour beverage made from fresh cucumbers, buttermilk, and a bit of sour cream, at times enriched with mint for twice the refreshment. After a quick taste, I opted to purchase a few more jugs to take back to the antique shop, where an old map awaited professional restoration by my gentle, trained hand.

◄———— **MAKES 4 SERVINGS** ————►

1 English cucumber, peeled and finely grated

4 tsp granulated sugar, or as needed

1 tsp kosher salt

2½ cups / 600ml buttermilk or plain kefir, cold, or as needed

2 Tbsp sour cream

1 Tbsp finely chopped fresh dill

Leaves from a few sprigs of mint, finely chopped (optional)

1 tsp apple cider vinegar, or as needed

Freshly ground black pepper

———◇———

In a medium bowl, combine the cucumber, sugar, and salt. Cover and let sit for 10 minutes to allow the cucumber to release some of its liquid. Add the buttermilk, sour cream, dill, and mint (if using) and stir to combine. Stir in the vinegar and season with pepper. Adjust the sweet/sour balance to your preference by adding more sugar or vinegar. If the drink is too thick, add more buttermilk.

Store the cooler in an airtight container in the fridge for up to 2 days. Serve chilled.

VARIATION: For a light sauce option to serve with cooked potatoes and meat, shred or thinly slice the cucumber instead of grating and omit the buttermilk to achieve a thicker consistency. Decrease the amount of sugar to ½ tsp, add only a few drops of vinegar, season with salt and pepper, and then garnish with some chopped dill.

OXENFURT

Redanian Fish Soup

Gossip is known to fly like the wind. Yet it passes even more swiftly along Oxenfurt's thoroughfares. In one instance, there were rumors of a vampire roaming the city streets. Folk wisdom on one's best defense against a bloodsucker has long been passed down by word of mouth. Debates continue over the relative merits of a stake through the heart versus a swift blow with a wagon axle to the demon's head. Oxenfurt's chefs proved particularly ingenious at one point when they opted to take matters into their own skilled hands. Following another well-known superstition, they added vast amounts of garlic to their menus, creating distinctive, memorable dishes. My personal favorites include a filling fish soup served by a chef who runs a kitchen down by the docks. Made with onion, carrot, parsley, and celery, heavily enriched with aromatic garlic perfectly complementing flavorful tomatoes, this simple soup requires no straining thanks to the inclusion of filleted fish—a trick the resourceful chef had learned from an herbalist he had met in Dillingen.

MAKES 4 SERVINGS

¼ cup / 60ml extra-virgin olive oil or vegetable oil
1 shallot or small onion, diced
2 celery stalks, diced
1 carrot, peeled and shredded
1 parsley root or parsnip, peeled and shredded
Kosher salt
4 garlic cloves, minced
¾ cup / 180ml dry white wine
1 cup / 240g tomato purée or strained tomatoes
1 bay leaf
4 cups / 960ml vegetable stock
Freshly ground black pepper
12 oz / 350g salmon or cod fillet, skinless
¼ cup / 15g chopped fresh dill, with more for garnishing
Fresh bread for serving

In a medium stockpot over medium heat, warm the olive oil. Add the shallot, celery, carrot, parsley root, and a pinch of salt and cook, stirring frequently, until the vegetables are softened, 4 to 5 minutes. Add the garlic and stir-fry for 30 seconds. Turn the heat to low, pour in the wine, and let simmer for 1 minute. Add the tomato purée, bay leaf, and vegetable stock. Turn the heat to medium and bring the soup to a boil, then turn the heat to low, cover, and let simmer until the vegetables are tender, about 30 minutes. Season with salt and pepper.

Meanwhile, pull out any pin bones from the salmon and then cut the flesh into 1¼-inch / 3cm cubes. Put the cubes and dill into the pot, cover, and let simmer until the fish is cooked through, about 5 minutes.

Pour the hot soup into bowls, garnish with chopped dill, and serve with hunks of bread.

Wedding Sweet Buns

A good wedding is about the fare and refreshments—a lesson I've learned countless times, as my own palate is my witness. While I was in Oxenfurt, my relations from Vizima invited me to join them at the wedding of a family friend. I couldn't resist the opportunity to bid Oxenfurt farewell at a grand celebration. The wedding took place at a charming country residence, its grounds amply decorated with wildflower garlands. Many symbolic wedding traditions meant to bring luck to the newlyweds were observed. The feast included a special wedding dessert called a *korowaj*, in this case served, not quite in line with tradition, in the form of smaller buns. The fluffy yeast-leavened buns made from milk, eggs, honey, and butter hid a smooth cheese filling enriched with dried fruit bits soaked in mead. When preparing this treat, it is traditionally good practice to use water drawn from seven rivers and milk from the best cow in the village. However, even without these particular ingredients, it is enough to follow one simple rule: make sure to bake the sweet buns a day before the wedding.

MAKES 8 BUNS

HONEY YEAST STARTER

2½ tsp instant yeast, or 25g fresh yeast, crumbled

3 Tbsp whole milk, at room temperature

1 tsp floral honey

2 Tbsp all-purpose flour

—

4/5 cup / 200ml whole milk, at room temperature

3 Tbsp floral honey

1 Tbsp granulated sugar

7 Tbsp / 100g melted unsalted butter, lukewarm

2 eggs

3¼ cups / 450g all-purpose flour, with more for sprinkling

½ cup / 60g medium rye flour

½ tsp kosher salt

CHEESE FILLING

½ cup / 60g raisins

¼ cup / 60ml mead or apple juice

14 oz / 400g Eskel's Tvorog (page 239) or light cream cheese

½ cup / 100g granulated sugar

2 egg yolks

2 tsp potato starch

—

1 egg, whisked

2 Tbsp chopped nuts (such as walnuts; optional)

TO MAKE THE STARTER: In a large bowl, combine the yeast, milk, and honey and stir until the yeast is dissolved. Then add the all-purpose flour and stir until smooth. Cover the bowl with a kitchen towel and set aside in a warm place until the starter has doubled in volume, 15 to 20 minutes.

In the bowl with the starter, add milk, honey, sugar, butter, and eggs and, using a fork, stir to incorporate. Add both flours and the salt and stir just until this dough is combined.

Lightly flour a work surface.

Transfer the dough to the prepared surface and, using your hands, knead the dough until it's smooth and elastic, about 3 minutes. If the dough is too sticky, sprinkle

Recipe continues

both the dough and the work surface with more all-purpose flour and continue kneading. Form the dough into a ball, sprinkle with more all-purpose flour, cover with the kitchen towel, and let rise at room temperature, until it has doubled in size, 1½ to 2 hours.

TO MAKE THE FILLING: In a small bowl, combine the raisins and mead and set aside to soak.

In a medium bowl, using a fork, mash the tvorog.

In a small bowl, using a whisk, cream together the sugar and egg yolks, then add to the bowl with the tvorog, add the potato starch, and whisk until combined. Strain the raisins and stir into the filling.

Line a baking sheet with parchment paper.

Divide the dough into two portions and, using a rolling pin, roll each piece into a 16 by 14-inch / 40 by 35cm rectangle, about ⅕ inch / 0.5cm thick, then cut into five 3 by 14-inch / 8 by 35cm strips. Spread the center of each strip with the filling, leaving a border of about ¾ inch / 2cm from each side. Bring the long edges together and seal them by dabbing with a little water and pinching the edges together. Repeat on the short edges. Twist each log into a spiral, folding and pressing the end of the strip to the bottom so the shape holds. Place the buns on the prepared baking sheet, cover with a kitchen towel, and let sit until almost doubled in size, about 40 minutes.

Preheat the oven to 350°F / 180°C.

Brush the top of the pastries with the egg and sprinkle with the nuts (if using).

Bake the pastries until nicely browned on top, about 45 minutes. Check after 25 minutes; if browning too quickly, tent with aluminum foil. Remove the pastries from the oven, transfer to a wire rack, and let cool for about 40 minutes before serving.

Festive Sausage Stew
with Potato Dumplings

The wedding festivities continued past midnight, the guests ever in high spirits thanks to stalls full of meat, bread, and other delicacies. All these paired perfectly with homemade vodka brought in by the crateload. Among all the fragrant foods served that night, one dish in particular caught my attention. I was encouraged to try it by the recipe's originator, who happened also to be the mother of the bride. While the rest of the party observed the newlyweds perform yet another fanciful ritual, I sat focused on a bowl of steaming potato dumplings. Slightly sticky, they were doused in an aromatic, brown sauce of smoked sausage, mushrooms, brined cucumbers, and a secret ingredient: plum jam. As the newlyweds strove to eat with their four hands tied together—another custom meant to bind them for life—I was quite content to busy my own hands with clearing my bowl. So sad it seemed to me when emptied that I began to ponder seconds at once . . .

———— ◆ MAKES 4 SERVINGS ◆ ————

POTATO DUMPLINGS

3 medium potatoes, peeled

Kosher salt

¾ cup / 140g potato starch, or as needed

—

2 Tbsp vegetable oil

10½ oz / 300g smoked kielbasa, sliced or cubed

1 large yellow onion, diced

9 oz / 250g button mushrooms, sliced

1½ cups / 360ml vegetable stock or water, or as needed

2 juniper berries, slightly crushed

1 bay leaf

2 Brined Cucumbers (page 83), drained, sliced or cubed

2 Tbsp unsalted butter

1½ Tbsp all-purpose flour

3 Tbsp plum jam, or as needed

¼ cup / 15g chopped fresh flat-leaf parsley

Kosher salt and freshly ground black pepper

TO MAKE THE DUMPLINGS: In a medium saucepan over medium heat, combine the potatoes and enough water to cover. Add 1 tsp salt, bring to a boil, cover, and cook until tender, about 40 minutes. Drain and set aside for 5 minutes to let the potatoes steam a bit. Using a potato masher, mash thoroughly and then season with ½ tsp salt. Set aside to cool to room temperature.

Transfer the cooled mashed potatoes onto a plate and flatten into a uniform circle using a spoon. Traditionally, this next step is done without measuring by replacing ¼ of the mashed potatoes with potato starch, using the following technique. Create an empty wedge of space in the mashed potato circle by scooping out one-fourth of the potatoes and setting them aside. Add enough potato starch to fill the space, then return the potatoes you just scooped out. Knead the potatoes and starch until well combined. If the dough is too sticky, add more potato starch; if it's too dry, add 1 to 2 Tbsp water.

Recipe continues

Divide the dough into walnut-size portions and form into balls. Using your palms, gently flatten each ball into a thick disk and, using your little finger or the end of a wooden spoon, make a slight hollow in the middle.

In a medium heavy saucepan over medium heat, warm the vegetable oil. Add the kielbasa and cook, stirring occasionally, until lightly browned, about 3 minutes. Add the onion and continue to cook, stirring occasionally, until browned, about 10 minutes more. Add the mushrooms and cook, stirring occasionally and scraping up the browned bits with a wooden spoon, until browned, about 5 minutes. Turn the heat to low, then add 1 cup / 240ml of the vegetable stock, the juniper berries, and bay leaf; cover; and let simmer, stirring occasionally, for 15 minutes. Add the brined cucumbers and let simmer for 10 minutes more.

Meanwhile, in a small nonstick skillet over medium-high heat, melt the butter. Add the flour and cook, stirring vigorously, until the flour is well browned,

about 5 minutes. Then add the remaining ½ cup / 120ml vegetable stock, stir vigorously to combine, turn the heat to low, and bring to a simmer. While stirring constantly, pour the mixture into the pan with the kielbasa. Add the plum jam and parsley, stir, and continue to simmer until thick, 4 to 5 minutes. If needed, add more vegetable stock and season with salt and pepper. Turn off the heat and discard the juniper berries and bay leaf.

While the stew simmers, in a large saucepan over medium-high heat, bring 2 qt / 2L of water to a boil. Add 1 Tbsp salt, stir, turn the heat to medium, and gently add the dumplings. Cook, gently stirring once or twice with a wooden spoon, until the dumplings float to the surface. Turn the heat to medium-low and let simmer until the dumplings are tender, about 4 minutes, then drain.

Place the dumplings in individual bowls, ladle in the warm stew, and serve immediately.

NOVIGRAD

Greeted by its towering city gates and the snap of heraldic banners fluttering in the wind, I arrived in this most famous metropolis in the North. The largest trading port on any shore of the Great Sea, the Free City of Novigrad stands proudly astride the Pontar River delta in the kingdom of Redania. There, breezes from the docks and fish market mingle with the rich smell of spices and pastries from market stalls. Together, they create a tangle of sweet-and-salty aromas that crisscross like trade winds in the city's muddy alleys and cobbled streets. These tendrils of scent meander past granaries, port cranes and soaring tenements housing powerful merchant and craft guilds. Finally, they reach the heart of the city—the bustling market square. If it's a feast you seek, the Golden Sturgeon, the Kingfisher, the Spear Blade and the acclaimed Chameleon are happy to oblige. In each of these establishments, troubadours' ballads blend with the clinking of gold coins and pewter cups. And they are just a few of the many eateries, taverns, inns and canteens that entice visitors. It would be a shame not to step through their heavy oak doors, where culinary treasures and exceptional flavors await! From the Continent's farthest reaches, no less!

The Spear Blade Inn's Onion Pottage

Of the thirty-five inns in the Free City of Novigrad, I chose the Kingfisher for my lodgings. It's rather hard to miss the brick building in Novigrad's market square, as a bright signboard proudly presents the inn's namesake bird with its vivid blue plumage. Given the inn's popularity and exceptional reputation in matters artistic and culinary, I simply could not deny myself the pleasure, though I knew my coin purse would suffer for it. Nevertheless, having arrived in the Free City around lunchtime, the aroma of onion soup soon drew me to a different establishment—The Spear Blade. The inn's patrons, preoccupied with rumors of a certain imp troubling the local merchants (a city-dwelling doppler, some suspected), abandoned their speculations when a simmering cauldron containing a fragrant golden liquid appeared in the dining room. The thick, hearty soup made from stale, leftover bread was full of melted cheese. And fried onion strings dangled from the guests' spoons with every bite.

MAKES 4 SERVINGS

2 Tbsp unsalted butter

2½ cups / 100g cubed sourdough bread
  (such as wheat or rye)

2½ cups / 600ml vegetable stock,
  beef stock, or water, or as needed

2 Tbsp vegetable oil

3 medium yellow onions, thinly sliced

Kosher salt

1 Tbsp floral honey

3 Tbsp water

1 sprig thyme, leaves picked, with more for
  garnishing, or ½ tsp dried thyme

Freshly ground black pepper

2 oz / 60g cheese (such as Gouda or Edam), grated

In a medium nonstick skillet over medium heat, melt 1 Tbsp of the butter. Add the bread and cook, stirring occasionally, until browned, about 5 minutes. Transfer these croutons to a medium saucepan, add the vegetable stock, and bring to a boil. Then turn the heat to low and let simmer, covered, stirring occasionally, for 15 minutes.

Pour the mixture through a fine-mesh sieve and, using a wooden spoon, press as much liquid as possible from the bread, then pour the liquid back into the saucepan. Set over low heat and let simmer while you cook the onion. Discard the bread residue left in the sieve.

In the same skillet over medium-high heat, warm the vegetable oil. Add the onion and 2 pinches of salt and cook, stirring occasionally with a wooden spoon, until the onion is softened and translucent, about 5 minutes. Add the honey and 3 Tbsp water and continue to cook

Recipe continues

for 25 minutes, stirring occasionally, until the onion is well browned. Add small splashes of water and scrape the bottom of the pan whenever the onion starts to stick. Add the remaining 1 Tbsp butter and stir-fry for 3 minutes more. Scoop out about 1 Tbsp of the onion, place in a small bowl, cover, and set aside. Add a splash of vegetable stock to the pan and deglaze, scraping up the browned bits with the wooden spoon, and transfer the remaining onion to the saucepan.

Add the thyme to the saucepan, stir, turn the heat to medium, and bring to a boil. Turn the heat to low and let simmer, stirring occasionally, for about 15 minutes. Season with salt and pepper. Add more stock or water if needed so that the soup is brothy and not too thick and let simmer for 5 minutes more.

Pour the hot soup into individual bowls, garnish each with grated cheese, a sprinkling of the reserved fried onion, a few thyme leaves, and a pinch of pepper. Serve immediately.

The Seven Cats' Brined Cucumber Soup

My horse Popiel, so kindly lent to me by my relatives in Vizima, was my faithful companion on the roads and trails of the North. So naturally, my daily routine in Novigrad included a visit to the city stables, where Popiel was quartered. I would then go to dine at a different tavern each day, hoping to try a new local delicacy. The dish in question came highly recommended by a group of halflings from the Meiersdorf Meadworks—that is to say, I overheard them loudly praising the brined cucumber soup at the Seven Cats Inn as they passed the stables. I had no choice but to taste it for myself! On my way, I passed a mess of broken glass and sweet cherry preserves spread across a paved alley—evidently heaved there from the second floor of a nearby tenement house in the heat of some quarrel. This sticky situation aside, my journey passed uneventfully. Upon my arrival at the Seven Cats, I ordered a deep dish of the unusual decoction, tiptoeing to a table so as not to spill even a drop of the fragrant liquid. The tangy, greenish pickled cucumber broth was rounded out with pieces of delicate meat, creamy potatoes, sweet carrots, and a dash of aromatic dill. It proved a true pleasure, a refreshing departure from some other soups I'd had the misfortune to try in the city. Woe to those who serve things excruciatingly bland.

MAKES 4 SERVINGS

14 oz / 400g pork ribs or shoulder

6 cups / 1.4L water

Kosher salt

5 black peppercorns

2 allspice berries

1 bay leaf

1 carrot

9 oz / 250g potatoes, peeled and cubed

1 Tbsp unsalted butter

5 drained Brined Cucumbers (page 83), shredded, plus brine, as needed (optional)

3 Tbsp heavy cream (optional)

¼ cup / 15g chopped fresh dill, with more for garnishing

Freshly ground black pepper

Fresh bread for dipping

In a large stockpot over low heat, combine the pork and water, and bring to a simmer. Using a slotted spoon, skim off and discard any accumulated foam from the surface. Add 1 tsp salt, the peppercorns, allspice berries, and bay leaf to the pot, cover, and let simmer for 1½ hours. Add the carrot and continue to cook until the meat is completely tender, about 30 minutes more.

Strain the stock and return to the pot. Transfer the meat to a plate and let cool slightly. If using pork ribs, peel the meat off the bones. Cut the pork into small chunks and set aside. Discard the bones and fat. Cube the carrot and set aside.

Add the potatoes and 1 tsp salt to the stock, bring to a simmer, and continue to cook until the potatoes are almost completely tender, about 15 minutes.

Recipe continues

Meanwhile, in a medium nonstick skillet over medium-high heat, melt the butter. Add the cucumbers and cook, stirring frequently, for 3 minutes. Transfer the cucumbers into the pot with the potatoes. Then add the cooked meat and carrot and let simmer for 15 minutes. Add the cream (if using), stir, and let simmer for 2 minutes more. Turn off the heat, add the dill, season with salt, if needed, and pepper. Taste, and if the soup isn't sour enough, add a splash of cucumber brine.

Pour the hot soup into individual bowls, garnish with dill, and serve with fresh bread for dipping.

Ofieri Spiced Chicken and Pumpkin Stew

The port crane on Novigrad's wharf sits nestled among warehouses and very near a tavern that boasts an extraordinary cook behind its modest counter. Having for years plied his trade on merchant ships, the cook then settled in the city to serve various dishes inspired by the faraway realms he had visited. I quickly became a regular, specifically after realizing that rarely would I spot the same dish on the menu twice. One day, an unfamiliar and intense fragrance as well as the cook's insistence bade me try a freshly prepared chicken and pumpkin stew. My bowl, filled to the brim, arrived flanked by pieces of warm flatbread, perfect for swiping up the aromatic sauce. The distinct, piquant taste of exotic spices suggested that an Ofieri ship had arrived in port. Seated among the dockworkers at mealtime, I took another spoonful, reflecting that, while the dishes served at the tavern tended toward the extravagant, they also provided a welcome window into the cuisines of distant lands.

───── ◄ MAKES 4 SERVINGS ► ─────

5 Tbsp / 75ml vegetable oil

1 medium red onion, diced

1¼ lb / 570g pumpkin, peeled, seeded,
    cut into ¾-inch / 2cm cubes

Kosher salt

3 garlic cloves, minced

4 tsp Ofieri Spice Blend (page 118), or as needed

2 oz / 60g kale leaves, fresh or frozen,
    stems and midribs removed

One 13.5-oz / 400ml can unsweetened coconut milk

10 oz / 300g boneless, skinless chicken breasts,
    cut into ¾-inch / 2cm cubes

3 Tbsp lemon juice, or as needed

1½ Tbsp floral honey, or as needed

2 Tbsp toasted pumpkin seeds, chopped (see Note)

Bring a kettle of water to a boil.

In a large nonstick skillet over medium heat, warm 3 Tbsp of the vegetable oil. Add the onion and cook, stirring frequently, for 3 minutes. Add the pumpkin cubes, sprinkle with 2 pinches of salt, and cook until lightly brown, about 5 minutes. Stir in the garlic and half of the spice blend and stir-fry for 1 minute. Transfer the contents of the skillet to a medium saucepan. Set the skillet aside without cleaning it.

Put the kale leaves in a colander, rinse with the boiling water, coarsely chop, and then transfer to the saucepan. Set over low heat, add the coconut milk and 1 tsp salt, cover, and bring to a simmer. Cook until the pumpkin is just tender, 30 to 40 minutes.

Recipe continues

Sprinkle the chicken with the remaining spice blend and 2 pinches of salt. Set the reserved skillet over medium heat and warm the remaining 2 Tbsp vegetable oil. Add the chicken and cook for 1 minute on each side. Add 3 Tbsp of cooking liquid from the saucepan, stir, and deglaze, scraping up the browned bits with a wooden spoon. Add the chicken and pan juices to the saucepan and let simmer, uncovered, until the chicken is cooked through, 5 minutes more.

Just before serving, stir in the lemon juice and honey. If necessary to balance the flavor, add more lemon juice, honey, spice blend, and salt.

Serve the stew hot, garnished with the toasted pumpkin seeds.

NOTE: To toast pumpkin seeds, put them in a small, dry nonstick skillet over medium heat, shaking the pan a few times, until lightly browned. Watch carefully as they can pop out of the pan and can also burn easily. Remove from the heat and let cool.

OFIERI SPICE BLEND
Makes 8 1/2 teaspoons

2 tsp ground turmeric
2 tsp ground cumin
1 tsp ground cinnamon
1 tsp ground coriander
1 tsp ground ginger
1 tsp chili powder or red pepper flakes
½ tsp ground cloves

In a small bowl, add the turmeric, cumin, cinnamon, coriander, ginger, pepper, and cloves, and stir until well combined.

Transfer to an airtight container and store in a cool, dry place for up to 1 month.

Roasted Chicken Drumsticks

Lady Luck is fickle indeed! I had the good fortune to unearth a copy of *My Evening with a Vampyre*—an exceedingly rare novel—at the Hodgson family's bookstore. Yet my discovery made me late for dinner at the Kingfisher. When at last I arrived, the "Battle of the Bards" I had seen promoted on posters throughout the city was well underway. The dining room was exceptionally yet understandably crowded. And the Kingfisher's most favored dishes had already disappeared from the bill of fare. Fortunately, one remained that I had overlooked (quite unfairly, I should add)—the chicken drumsticks. Marinated in buttermilk with garlic and herbs, they are then golden roasted and served with a spicy dipping sauce.

— MAKES 4 SERVINGS ➤

HERBED BUTTERMILK MARINADE
1 cup / 240ml buttermilk
2 garlic cloves, minced
2 tsp kosher salt
1 tsp dried tarragon
1 tsp dried rosemary
1 tsp dried thyme
—
2¼ lb / 1kg chicken drumsticks
Vegetable oil for brushing
1 tsp dried tarragon

DIPPING SAUCE
3 Tbsp mayonnaise
2 Tbsp floral honey
1½ tsp spicy mustard
½ tsp mixed peppercorns, coarsely ground
2 pinches kosher salt

In a large bowl, combine the buttermilk, garlic, salt, tarragon, rosemary, and thyme. Add the drumsticks to the marinade and coat thoroughly. Cover and refrigerate for 12 to 24 hours, tossing twice.

About 40 minutes before baking, remove the drumsticks from the fridge and let sit at room temperature to take the chill off. Preheat the oven to 400°F / 200°C. Brush a 13 by 9-inch / 33 by 23cm baking dish with vegetable oil.

Discard the marinade and place the drumsticks in the prepared dish, arranging them skin-side up about 1 inch / 3cm apart. Brush each drumstick with a little vegetable oil and sprinkle with the tarragon.

Bake the drumsticks, uncovered, for 15 minutes, cover with aluminum foil or a lid, and then turn the oven temperature to 325°F / 165°C. Continue baking until the drumsticks are completely tender, about 50 minutes; baste with the cooking juices two or three times. Then remove the foil, turn the oven temperature to 425°F / 220°C, and continue to bake until the skin is nicely browned, about 15 minutes.

TO MAKE THE DIPPING SAUCE: While the drumsticks are baking, in a small bowl, combine the mayonnaise, honey, mustard, peppercorns, and salt. Stir to incorporate, and then cover and place in the fridge until ready to serve.

Remove the drumsticks from the oven and let rest for 5 minutes, and then transfer to a serving plate. Serve with the dipping sauce on the side.

Harborside Zander in Thyme

Served at the Golden Sturgeon, this fish specialty came recommended to me entirely by chance. A dwarf witnessed my hesitation as I perused the inn's menu. As luck would have it, he was a member of the Pride of the Pontar, a fishing club. He claimed he would be delighted to introduce me to the chef's creations and to the vagaries of the local competitive rod-fishing scene. The latter he detailed in an amusing and eloquent manner, particularly when enumerating the rules of the tournament code, set down following numerous brawls during which fishing gear had been used quite contrary to its intended purpose. I also learned what became of the fish caught during competitions. The winning fish each year is deemed "King of the Pontar" and ceremonially released back into the river's waters, while Novigrad's innkeepers buy the rest of the day's catch to then use it in creating new recipes to commemorate the event. One such recipe, the Golden Sturgeon's zander in thyme, served in a skillet with a creamy sauce of stewed leeks and white wine, has won recognition among the inn's regular clientele and become a staple of the menu. The dish does much to discredit the rather vulgar, unfavorable opinion, popular in some (rival?) circles, that zander tastes like "soaped-up shite."

◀ MAKES 4 SERVINGS ▶

Four 3½-oz / 100g skin-on zander, trout, or cod fillets
1 cup / 240ml whole milk
2 leeks (white and green parts), trimmed and halved
3 Tbsp unsalted butter
½ cup / 120ml dry white wine
7 Tbsp / 100ml heavy cream
2 sprigs thyme, plus thyme leaves for garnishing
Kosher salt and freshly ground black pepper
½ tsp dried thyme

Arrange the fish fillets in a shallow baking dish, pour in the milk, cover, and refrigerate for 1 hour, turning once. While the fillets are in the fridge, rinse the leeks thoroughly, then drain and thinly slice.

Drain the fillets, discard the milk, and gently pat the fish dry on each side with paper towels. Set aside, uncovered.

In a medium saucepan over medium heat, melt 2 Tbsp of the butter. Add the leeks and cook, stirring occasionally,

until soft, about 5 minutes. Add the wine and cook until the liquid evaporates, about 5 minutes. Add the cream and thyme sprigs and season with salt and pepper, then turn the heat to low and let simmer, stirring frequently, until this sauce thickens, about 5 minutes. Turn off the heat, remove the thyme sprigs, cover, and set aside.

Sprinkle the fish fillets on both sides with salt and pepper and the dried thyme.

In a large nonstick skillet over medium heat, melt the remaining 1 Tbsp butter. Add the fillets, skin-side down, and cook for 2 minutes. Then gently flip the fillets and continue to cook for about 3 minutes more, until the flesh is well set and lightly browned on the surface.

Spoon a generous portion of the sauce onto serving plates, then top with the fillets, and garnish with chopped thyme leaves. Serve immediately.

Hattori's Redanian Red Lentil Dumplings

At first, I would easily lose my way in the largest metropolis in the North, its towering buildings, bustling markets, and busy squares blending into a nameless blur. With time, however, I began to identify various patterns. In observing the daily routines of the city's inhabitants, I noted a place where city guards, students, and any better-informed visitors converged throughout the day, dawn to dusk. Located under an inconspicuous wooden roof, the establishment combined two seemingly unrelated crafts—cooking and blacksmithing. Despite having two entrances, the enterprise operates under a shared name: Hattori's Swords and Dumplings. Its eponymous founder, an elf known far and wide for his smithing skills, tempered his fascination with cooking by running a thriving dumpling business alongside his forge. When placing my order, I hesitated—Redanian or Mariborian? The former won out. I found the boiled dumplings captivating for their savory filling made of red lentils, onions, and Ofieri spices, all wrapped in a springy, toothsome dough and topped with butter-fried garlic and parsley. So despite my initial hesitation, once eating I was sure I'd made the best possible choice . . .

MAKES ABOUT 20 DUMPLINGS

BOILED DUMPLING DOUGH
½ cup / 120ml hot water
1 cup / 140g all-purpose flour, with more for sprinkling
1 Tbsp vegetable oil
½ tsp kosher salt

FILLING
1 cup / 240ml water
½ cup / 90g split red lentils, rinsed
Kosher salt
1 Tbsp vegetable oil
1 small onion, diced
½ tsp Ofieri Spice Blend (page 118; optional)
Freshly ground black pepper
—
Kosher salt

TOPPING
2 Tbsp unsalted butter
1 garlic clove, minced
Kosher salt
Several sprigs flat-leaf parsley, chopped

TO MAKE THE DOUGH: In a small saucepan over medium-high heat, bring the water to a boil. Then turn off the heat and set aside to cool for 5 minutes.

In a medium bowl, combine the flour, vegetable oil, salt, and hot water. Using a fork, stir to roughly combine, let cool for about 1 minute (until you can easily touch it with bare hands), and then knead in the bowl until uniform and smooth. If the dough is too sticky, sprinkle it with a little flour. Once the dough is well combined, form it into a ball, cover with an upside-down metal bowl, and set aside for 30 minutes.

TO MAKE THE FILLING: In a medium saucepan over high heat, bring the water to a boil. Add the lentils, turn the heat to low, partially cover, and let simmer, stirring occasionally, until all the water has evaporated, about 15 minutes. The lentils should be completely soft but not runny, with a thick and mushy texture. Uncover, turn off the heat, and stir in ½ tsp salt.

In a medium nonstick skillet over medium-high heat, warm the vegetable oil. Add the onion and cook, stirring frequently, until lightly browned, about 5 minutes. Turn off the heat and transfer the onion into the saucepan with the lentils. Using a fork or a potato masher, mash well and then set aside to cool. Add the spice blend (if using) and a generous grinding of pepper and stir to combine. The filling should be well seasoned, but if needed, add more salt.

Sprinkle a work surface with flour. Divide the dough in half and, using a rolling pin, roll out one portion 1⁄16 inch / 2mm thick. Using a 3-inch / 7cm round cookie cutter, cut out ten circles. Roll out the scraps with the remaining dough and repeat to cut out another ten circles. Place a heaping 1 tsp of the filling in the center of each

circle, then fold the dough to make a half-moon and pinch the edges together to seal. To add a decorative frill to the edges, use your thumb and forefinger to seal. Cover the dumplings with a kitchen towel so they don't dry out.

Set a large saucepan of water over high heat and bring to a boil. Add 2 tsp salt and stir, then turn the heat to medium and add half of the dumplings. After 1 minute, stir gently with a wooden spoon and let simmer until they float to the surface, about 5 minutes. Continue to simmer, until the dumplings are soft, about 3 minutes. Using a slotted spoon, transfer to a platter and continue cooking the remaining dumplings.

TO MAKE THE TOPPING: While the dumplings are cooking, in a small saucepan over low heat, melt the butter. Add the garlic and a pinch of salt, turn the heat to low, and cook, stirring frequently, until lightly browned, about 1 minute. Turn off the heat, add the parsley, and stir to combine. Set aside.

Once all the dumplings have been cooked, pour the topping over them, and serve immediately.

NOVIGRAD

Hattori's Mariborian Baked Mushroom Dumplings

. . . That is, until a few days later, when I resolved to try the Mariborian variety. A painful culinary dilemma if ever I've faced one! The crispy, buttery dough sprinkled with nigella seeds hid a filling of aromatic mushrooms, onions, parsley leaves, as well as wild garlic—a personal favorite. Thereafter, I made sure to order the baked dumplings several more times, using each such opportunity to question the elven waitress about the particular ingredients used. Based on my culinary interrogations, I managed to draft my own version of the recipe, which I hope captures the unique flavor of this fantastic dish. Each time I left Hattori's, belly full and thus cheerful, I promised myself I would persuade my family in Kovir to make the dumplings a staple of our menu there.

MAKES ABOUT 15 DUMPLINGS

BAKED DUMPLING DOUGH

1 cup / 140g all-purpose flour, with more for sprinkling
½ cup / 60g whole-wheat flour
7 Tbsp / 100g unsalted butter, cold and cut up
⅓ cup / 80ml sour cream
½ tsp kosher salt

FILLING

1½ oz / 40g dried mushroom slices
  (such as bay bolete or porcini)
1 Tbsp vegetable oil
1 medium yellow onion, diced
1 Tbsp unsalted butter
2 Tbsp chopped fresh flat-leaf parsley
1½ Tbsp dried bread crumbs, or as needed
½ tsp dried wild garlic (optional)
Kosher salt and freshly ground black pepper

—

1 egg, beaten
1 tsp nigella seeds
½ tsp dried wild garlic or dried chives
Sour cream for serving (optional)

TO MAKE THE DOUGH: In a medium bowl, using your fingers, rub together both flours and the butter until the mixture is the consistency of bread crumbs. Add the sour cream and salt and knead just until combined. If the dough is too sticky, sprinkle with a little all-purpose flour. Form the dough into a ball, cover the bowl with a kitchen towel, and refrigerate for 45 minutes.

TO MAKE THE FILLING: Rinse the mushroom slices under cold water, transfer to a small bowl, cover with lukewarm water, and let soak for 1 hour. Add the mushrooms and their soaking liquid to a small saucepan and simmer until tender, about 30 minutes. Then strain the mushrooms and coarsely chop, reserving the cooking water.

In a medium nonstick skillet over medium heat, warm the vegetable oil. Add the onion and cook, stirring occasionally, until softened, about 5 minutes. Add the mushrooms and butter and continue to cook, stirring, until the onion and mushrooms are tender, about 3 minutes more. Add a few tablespoons of the reserved soaking water and let simmer until the water evaporates, about 4 minutes. Turn off the heat, add the parsley, bread crumbs, and wild garlic (if using) and stir thoroughly to combine. The filling should be moist and firm; add more bread crumbs if it is too runny. Season generously with salt and pepper.

Preheat the oven to 350°F / 180°C. Line a baking sheet with parchment paper. Sprinkle a work surface with all-purpose flour.

Remove the dough from the fridge and let sit at room temperature for about 5 minutes to take the chill off. Divide the dough in half and, using a rolling pin, roll out one portion ⅟₁₆ inch / 2mm thick. Using a 3-inch / 7cm round cookie cutter, cut out six circles. Roll out the scraps with the remaining dough and repeat to

cut out another seven circles. Place a heaping 1 tsp of the filling in the center of each circle, then fold the dough to make a half-moon and carefully pinch the edges together to seal. Press a fork into the edges of the dough to create a decorative frill and make sure the dumplings are fully sealed.

Place the dumplings on the prepared baking sheet, leaving a little space between each one. Brush the tops with a little of the beaten egg and sprinkle with the nigella seeds and wild garlic.

Bake the dumplings until the tops are golden brown, 20 to 25 minutes. These are best eaten while hot but may also be eaten at room temperature. Serve with sour cream if desired.

The Chameleon's Chilled Beetroot Soup

In their style and presentation, dishes served at the more elegant of Novigrad's taverns oft echo the establishments' decor and atmosphere, some unique aspect thereof. This was very much the case at the Chameleon. Paintings of the inn's owner, the famed bard Dandelion, a frequent visitor to royal courts, his work known from Toussaint to Poviss, were complemented by glass lanterns and rich crimson and magenta fabrics stretched across walls and beams. In guest alcoves thus adorned a similarly vibrant chilled beetroot soup was served on specially decorated tables. The dish, made on a buttermilk base then tinted light pink, featured sweet-and-sour notes that combined perfectly with freshly chopped beet greens, juicy radishes, and a soft-boiled egg. The Chameleon's patrons would indulge in feasts both culinary and spiritual, consuming the fine fare while enjoying the evening's entertainment. The latter oft explored urban legends, events reputed to have transpired in Novigrad's streets—including a sordid tale of a haunted tenement house, a secret treasure, the Prince of Thieves and the city's humble savior, the Crimson Avenger . . .

MAKES 4 SERVINGS

12 oz / 350g young beets, with leafy tops (see Note)
1 Tbsp vegetable oil
Kosher salt
1 Tbsp apple cider vinegar or lemon juice, or as needed
2 cups / 480ml buttermilk, cold
Generous ¾ cup plus 1½ Tbsp / 200ml sour cream
5 radishes, stemmed and diced
½ cup / 60g cucumber, peeled and grated
¼ cup / 15g chopped fresh dill, with more for garnishing
2½ Tbsp chopped fresh chives, with more for garnishing
½ cup / 60g raspberries (optional)
3 tsp granulated sugar, or as needed
Freshly ground black pepper
Soft-boiled eggs, halved, for serving

Thoroughly rinse the beets, especially between the leaves, under running water. Cut off the stems and leaves and finely chop them. Then peel the beets and cut them into 1-inch- / 2cm-long thin strips or finely dice.

In a medium saucepan over medium-high heat, warm the vegetable oil. Add the beets and fry, stirring occasionally for 5 minutes, then add enough water to cover (about 1½ cups / 360ml) and turn the heat to medium-low. Add two pinches of salt, bring to a gentle simmer, and cook until tender, about 10 minutes. Add the chopped stems and leaves and let simmer for 3 to 4 minutes. Add the vinegar and stir, then turn off the heat and let cool to room temperature. (To speed up the process, place the pan in a large bowl filled with cold water.)

Recipe continues

Add the buttermilk, sour cream, radishes, cucumber, dill, and chives to the beets and stir vigorously until well combined. Using a spoon, press the raspberries through a fine-mesh sieve over the pot (if using) and discard the seeds. Stir in the sugar and season with salt and pepper. Cover and refrigerate for 1 to 2 hours to let the flavors develop. Add a splash more of buttermilk if the soup is too thick, or more vinegar or sugar to balance the flavor.

Serve the soup, chilled, topped with the eggs and garnished with fresh dill and chives.

Store the soup in an airtight container in the fridge for up to 2 days.

NOTE: If young beets are difficult to find or are not in season, you can substitute an equal amount of peeled and shredded beets and cook as directed until tender. If desired, you can substitute young beet leaves with a handful of baby spinach.

NOVIGRAD

Doughnuts with Plum Jam and Bacon Sprinkles

One thing that never fails to lift my spirits or deliver a pleasant reprieve from my duties is a warm, fluffy doughnut. And never do I pass up the chance to try a new flavor. Topped with crunchy bacon bits, this variation on the dessert, specific to Novigrad, proved slightly richer than I'm accustomed to, but also tastier! Served from a small, family-run shop, these doughnuts filled with plum jam and fried in lard are made according to a recipe passed down over generations. The family enterprise began with a market stall in Gors Velen, offering sweets to all who passed, among them young enchantresses-in-training en route to Thanedd Island. The stand quickly grew into a shop. The enterprise continued to expand and soon the family's doughnuts began to appear in other cities as well. The Novigrad branch has proudly continued the family tradition, now offering not only sweet treats for sale, but also workshops for all lovers of the confectionery arts.

MAKES ABOUT 15 DOUGHNUTS

BUTTERMILK YEAST STARTER

2½ tsp instant yeast, or 25g fresh yeast, crumbled

1 tsp granulated sugar

3 Tbsp buttermilk, at room temperature

3 Tbsp all-purpose flour

—

3 Tbsp vegetable oil

½ cup / 120ml buttermilk, at room temperature

2½ cups / 350g all-purpose flour, with more for sprinkling

2 Tbsp granulated sugar

4 egg yolks

Kosher salt

1 Tbsp plain vodka

ICING

2¼ cups / 220g confectioners' sugar

¼ cup / 60ml water, or as needed

2 or 3 drops lemon juice

—

3½ oz / 100g slab bacon, thinly sliced

1 qt / 1L melted pork lard or vegetable oil (see Note)

Plum jam for filling

TO MAKE THE STARTER: In a medium bowl, combine the yeast, granulated sugar, and buttermilk and stir until the yeast is fully dissolved. Add the flour and mix with a fork until well combined. Cover the bowl with a kitchen towel and let the starter sit until doubled in size, 15 to 20 minutes.

Lightly flour a work surface.

Add the vegetable oil, buttermilk, flour, granulated sugar, egg yolks, and a pinch of salt to the bowl with the starter. Using a fork, stir together, then add the vodka and stir again to form a sticky dough. Transfer to the prepared work surface and knead for about 5 minutes. Sprinkle the dough with a little flour while kneading so it becomes smoother and less sticky at the end of the kneading process. Form the dough into a ball, cover with a kitchen towel, and let rise on the work surface until doubled in size, about 1½ hours.

Recipe continues

Line a baking sheet with parchment paper and then oil the parchment.

After the dough has doubled in size, punch it down and knead it a few times. Using a rolling pin, roll the dough into a rectangle or circle about ½ inch / 1.5cm thick. Using a 2½-inch / 6cm cookie cutter, cut out ten circles and transfer to the prepared baking sheet, spacing the circles 2 inches / 5cm apart. Re-roll the scraps and cut out another five circles. Cover the circles with a kitchen towel and let rise until almost doubled in size, about 20 minutes.

TO MAKE THE ICING: In a small bowl, whisk together the confectioners' sugar, water, and lemon juice until smooth and thick like sour cream. Set aside.

Line a plate with a double layer of paper towels.

In a medium nonstick skillet over medium heat, combine the bacon and a splash of cold water and cook, stirring occasionally, until the water evaporates, 2 to 3 minutes. Fry until the fat melts and the bacon is heavily browned on one side, about 4 minutes, then flip the strips and fry until the second side is browned, about 2 minutes more. Place the bacon on the prepared plate to drain, let cool for 2 minutes, and then coarsely chop into sprinkles. Transfer to a bowl and set aside.

Re-line the plate with a double layer of paper towels.

In a deep heavy saucepan, add enough lard to reach halfway up the sides and then set over medium heat for a few minutes. Check the temperature by submerging a pea-size ball of the dough in the lard; if it bubbles immediately and the dough becomes brown in 1 minute, then the oil is ready. If using an instant-read thermometer, the temperature should read 350°F / 180°C.

Place two dough circles in the oil, cover for 30 seconds, uncover, and continue to fry until nicely browned, 1 to 2 minutes on one side. Flip and fry on the other side; look for a pale, thin stripe to appear in the middle of each doughnut as an indicator that it is perfectly fried. Using a slotted spoon, transfer the fried doughnuts to the prepared plate to drain, 1 to 2 minutes, then dip each doughnut halfway in the bowl with the icing and place icing-side up on a wire rack. Scatter the bacon sprinkles on top of the icing.

Using a pastry bag with a tip, or a large syringe with a thick tip, squeeze 1 to 2 tsp of jam inside each doughnut. Let the doughnuts cool completely before serving.

NOTE: A 50/50 mixture of lard and vegetable oil gives the doughnuts a milder, lighter flavor.

Nilfgaardian Lemon

Like all good things, my sojourn in Novigrad eventually came to an end. I spent my final evening at the Nilfgaardian Embassy, at a reception to which I had somehow, and I know not by whom, been invited during a sumptuous dinner in Oxenfurt. Some fine canvasses by van Rogh were on display alongside an elegant tasting buffet. Among the delicacies, I spied a sunny-hued drink served in small, thimble glasses. Nilfgaardian lemon, as the hosts referred to it, delighted my palate with its hint of honey and touch of black pepper. How very refreshing! According to the embassy's chef, the bottles must absolutely be deeply chilled before serving. Later, a Nilfgaardian officer from Geso, circling the buffet, admitted (after having enjoyed more than a few glasses) that the tincture had originated in his native province, despite the Nilfgaardians' claim to the concoction. After all, the Empire's borders were continually expanding to include an ever-growing list of culinary traditions. The officer treated me to more stories as we emptied more glasses of the golden liquid. By evening's end, hours later, I found myself wandering back to the Kingfisher, my very own bottle of the lemon liqueur tucked under my arm, though I could not imagine how it had gotten there.

MAKES ABOUT 3¼ CUPS / 750ML

EXTRACT
5 medium lemons
2 cups / 480ml plain vodka (80 proof)
8 black peppercorns

SYRUP
Juice from 5 lemons (see above)
½ cup / 100g granulated sugar
¼ cup / 60g floral honey

TO MAKE THE EXTRACT: In a medium bowl, cover the lemons with lukewarm water. Set aside for 15 minutes, and then discard the water. Using a brush, rub the lemons thoroughly under warm running water. Pat dry with a kitchen towel. Using a vegetable peeler, remove the lemon zest (the yellow outer layer, not the spongy white pith underneath). Cover the lemons with a kitchen towel to keep them from drying out and set aside.

In a sterile 1-qt / 1L jar with a lid, pour in the vodka and add the lemon zest and peppercorns, cover, and shake to combine. Set aside at room temperature for 12 hours.

TO MAKE THE SYRUP: Roll the zested lemons on a tabletop with your palm, then cut in half and squeeze ¾ cup plus 2 Tbsp / 220ml juice through a fine-mesh sieve into a liquid measuring cup.

In a small saucepan over low heat, combine the lemon juice and sugar and cook, stirring until the sugar fully dissolves, about 2 minutes. Turn off the heat and let the mixture cool to lukewarm, then stir in the honey. Let cool completely.

Using the sieve, strain the alcohol extract, discarding the zest and peppercorns. Pour the syrup into the alcohol jar, then add the strained extract and, using a perfectly clean spoon, stir to combine. Cover and store at room temperature in a dark place for 3 days.

When ready to serve, strain the liquid through a coffee filter, discarding any remaining residue.

Store in an airtight container in the refrigerator for up to 4 weeks.

SKELLIGE ISLES

A violent tempest churned the sea. The briny spray and icy winds chilled me to the bone—a portent of the climes that awaited me. When those craggy cliffs emerged from the mist at long last, I knew I had reached my destination—a refuge anchored firmly amidst the swirling storm. I had been fortunate. The waves of the Great Sea surrounding the Skellige Isles are notoriously fickle guides for merchant ships from afar and local long-ships alike, known to the islanders as drakkars. For most inhabitants of the Continent, this archipelago off the coasts of Verden and Cintra might well be the edge of the world, a strange place shrouded in myth and legend. Though the Isles are indeed difficult to reach, once you arrive, the fog of superstition lifts quickly and you discover a land that is home to numerous proud, independent clans and many a boundless, breathtaking vista. From my brief time walking those rocky shores and heathered trails—gazing at cloud-draped mountains, snow-capped peaks and cliffsides swarmed by squawking gulls—I came to realize that the harsh conditions of the archipel-ago spare none. Not least a landlubber like myself. With windburned cheeks and frozen bones comes a wolfish appetite—something easily remedied in one of Skellige's many taverns. Often, while warming myself by a crackling fire, I learned just how many of their dishes celebrate the bounty of the sea. The cuisine of the Isles combines traditional, local ingredients with those brought there through raiding or maritime trade.

Hindarsfjall Lard Spread
with Apple and Onion

My stay in Novigrad had been exquisite. Its end proved more dispiriting than I had anticipated. Yet, knowing that my journey must continue, I bid farewell to Popiel, entrusting him to my uncle who would return him to the family's stables in Vizima. I then secured passage on a ship bound for An Skellig. Alas, once at sea, a powerful squall forced us to make landfall prematurely at Hindarsfjall. Wet to my knickers and bones shivering, I sought refuge in Larvik at an inn where a priestess of Freya soon arrived to offer aid. As my toes thawed over a warm hearth, my palate enjoyed freshly rendered lard with apple, onion, and cracklings, smeared atop a slice of rye bread. Paired with a warm drink, this hearty combination is considered a village specialty. Indeed, so special it was that I completely forgot about the tempest raging outside.

MAKES ABOUT 2¾ CUPS / 650G

14 oz / 400g skinless fatback, diced
5 oz / 150g slab bacon, diced
1 small onion, diced
1 small apple, peeled and shredded
1 tsp kosher salt
1 tsp dried marjoram
1 tsp dried wild garlic (optional)
Rye bread for serving

In a large skillet over medium heat, cook the fatback, stirring occasionally with a wooden spoon, until half of the fat has melted, about 20 minutes. The fat should be slightly bubbling; if it's too intense, lower the heat.

Add the bacon to the skillet and cook until most of the fat has melted and the cracklings are lightly browned, 15 to 25 minutes. Add the onion, apple, and salt and cook until the onion is golden, 8 to 12 minutes. Turn off the heat and set aside to slightly cool, about 15 minutes, then season with the marjoram and wild garlic (if using) and stir to combine.

Pour the contents of the skillet into a 4-cup / 950ml bowl and set aside at room temperature to cool. Store in an airtight container in the refrigerator for up to 2 weeks. Remove from the fridge about 30 minutes before serving to take the chill off.

Serve the spread with sliced rye bread.

Larvik Mulled Rivian Kriek

The warm drink served alongside my lard and rye was a mulled Rivian kriek—a ruby-colored, cherry-fruited beer with ginger. Although brewed in faraway Rivia, as the name indicates, a smattering of bottles still find their way to Hindarsfjall from time to time. But for periods when shipments are far and few between, these Skelligers devised a clever recipe for Larvik's own "kriek"—a dark beer combined with cherry syrup.

MAKES 1 SERVING

16 oz / 500ml dark beer
3 Tbsp cherry syrup, or as needed
3 slices peeled fresh ginger
Floral honey for sweetening (optional)

In a small saucepan over low heat, combine the beer, cherry syrup, and ginger and cook until hot and slightly steaming but not boiling. Turn off the heat and let sit for 2 minutes. Taste and sweeten with honey if desired.

Serve the kriek warm or at room temperature; it tastes good both ways.

VARIATIONS

For a more festive version, add a pinch of Zerrikanian Spice Blend (page 42) before serving.

For a raspberry version, replace the cherry syrup with raspberry syrup, which also pairs well with dark beer.

SKELLIGE ISLES

An Skellig Fish in Salt Crust
with Carrot and Mint Salad

Once the weather had improved enough for us to resume our journey, we set out from Hindarsfjall for the port of An Skellig. It was there I sought out a meal recommended to me during my time in Novigrad. With an eager belly, I quickly found my way through Urialla Harbor to a tavern known for this island's specialty—sturgeon roasted atop a sea-salt crust, served with a side of carrot shavings and mint. Alas, due to overfishing in the region, sturgeon had become a delicacy reserved for special occasions. So instead, I enjoyed the dish prepared with common trout. And yet . . . through this unique, salt-heavy roasting method, the trout's flavor was anything but common. Delicious, tender, juicy flesh with the fragrant aromas of dill, butter, pepper, and lemon—the plate's lone exotic ingredient, imported from the warmest corners of the Continent. Although the fish and salad delighted me with perfect balance, the salt crust delighted all others at my table. For handling the dish proved an embarrassingly messy spectacle, though not an experience I shall ever regret.

———— ✦ MAKES 2 SERVINGS ✦ ————

CARROT AND MINT SALAD
2 carrots, shredded
10 mint leaves, chopped
2 tsp floral honey
3 drops lemon juice
1 pinch kosher salt
1 pinch freshly ground black pepper

—

One 12 oz / 340g whole rainbow trout, gutted, head on
Kosher salt and freshly ground black pepper
4 tsp unsalted butter, thinly sliced
½ lemon, thinly sliced
4 sprigs dill
2¼ lb / 1kg coarse sea salt, with more for sprinkling
⅓ cup / 80ml cold water, or as needed

———— ◇ ————

TO MAKE THE SALAD: In a medium bowl, combine the carrots, mint, honey, lemon juice, kosher salt, and pepper and stir to incorporate. Cover and let sit for 30 minutes.

Wash both the outside and the cavity of the trout under running water. Thoroughly pat it dry with a paper towel. Sprinkle the cavity with kosher salt and pepper and then arrange the butter, lemon, and dill inside. Fold the opening closed, gently pressing the fish from both sides with your hands. Set aside.

Preheat the oven to 350°F / 180°C. Line a baking sheet with parchment paper.

In a large bowl, add the coarse sea salt and slowly stir in the water until the mixture is the consistency of wet sand. Spread half of the salt mixture in the center of the prepared baking sheet to create an even layer about ½ inch / 1.5cm thick and the length of the fish. Place the trout on the salt, then cover evenly with the remaining salt (leave the tail fin uncovered). Carefully pat the salt mound with your palm, making sure there are no gaps.

Recipe continues

Bake the fish until the salt crust is lightly browned, about 40 minutes. Remove from the oven and let rest until the crust cools a bit, about 5 minutes. Then, using a knife, break the crust near the fish head and gently unfold the skin to gain access to the meat.

Serve the fish immediately with the carrot salad.

NOTE: For diners unfamiliar with whole fish, guide them to first eat the meat from the top side of the fish, then use their fingers to remove the entire spine by pulling it up from the tail end in one steady move. They can then continue to eat the remaining fillet.

Svorlag Trapper Meat Patties
with Green Vegetables

From An Skellig I journeyed to Ard Skellig. Along the way I was afforded a unique opportunity— to admire the awe-inspiring cliffs and rockfaces that form the shoreline of this largest island of the archipelago. Before we reached Kaer Trolde, a longship hailed us, then pulled alongside. The mariners warned us of siren attacks along our route, so we changed course for the isle of Spikeroog. There we sailed into a charming bay, its waters kept calm by dense forests that surround it and the nearby village of Svorlag. Alas, as this unscheduled stop was due to be brief, we did not venture beyond the local tavern, where we travelers had accompanied our captain. I was immediately struck by the presence of local trappers, their trophies abundantly adorning the walls. I knew immediately the folk of Spikeroog would have more to offer than fish. Before long, I was enjoying the savory aroma and flavor of their signature meat-and-spinach patties served with fried miniature cabbages and a thick blueberry-plum jam. Meanwhile, at the neighboring table, villagers familiar with the archipelago's dangers advised our captain to take a new route to avoid both rough seas and sea monsters that prowl the waves.

MAKES 4 SERVINGS

4 Tbsp vegetable oil
1 medium onion, finely diced
Kosher salt
2 garlic cloves, minced
3½ oz / 100g spinach
2 pinches grated nutmeg
2 cups / 480ml water, or as needed
7 oz / 200g brussels sprouts
10 oz / 300g ground beef
7 oz / 200g ground pork
5 Tbsp dried bread crumbs
2 Tbsp / 10g Grana Padano or Parmesan, finely grated
Freshly ground black pepper
2 Tbsp all-purpose flour
1 tsp unsalted butter
1 tsp floral honey
1 tsp apple cider vinegar

PLUM–BLUEBERRY SAUCE
1 tsp unsalted butter
2 Tbsp plum jam
1 cup / 120g blueberries
Kosher salt
Floral honey for sweetening (optional)

In a large nonstick skillet over medium heat, warm 1 Tbsp of the vegetable oil. Add the onion and a pinch of salt, and cook, stirring occasionally, until slightly browned, about 5 minutes. Add the garlic and stir-fry for 30 seconds more. Add the spinach and another pinch of salt, stir, and cook until the water evaporates and the spinach has become soft, about 5 minutes. Season with the nutmeg, stir, transfer to a large bowl, and let cool to room temperature.

Recipe continues

Meanwhile, remove the outside leaves from the brussels sprouts and trim the stems. In a small saucepan over high heat, bring the water to a boil. Add 1 tsp salt and the brussels sprouts, turn the heat to low, and cook for 3 minutes. Drain, let off the steam, and halve lengthwise. Set aside.

Add the beef, pork, bread crumbs, cheese, 2 Tbsp water, 1 tsp salt, and a generous grinding of pepper to the bowl with the spinach and onion. Using your hands, knead the ingredients together, until the mass is well combined and moist. If it feels too dry, add a splash more water and knead to incorporate.

Put the flour into a medium bowl. Form the meat into 2-inch / 5cm balls, slightly flatten them into patties, and place in the flour to coat, shaking off the excess flour.

In a large nonstick skillet over medium-high heat, warm 2 Tbsp of the vegetable oil. Add the meat patties and cook until browned, about 3 minutes, then flip and cook the other side. Add 2 Tbsp water to the pan, shake, and cover with a lid. Turn the heat to medium-low and let simmer for about 5 minutes, flipping the patties twice. If the water evaporates, add another 1 to 2 Tbsp and continue to simmer. Remove the lid, turn the heat to high, and cook until nicely browned, 2 to 3 minutes on each side. Transfer the patties to a plate, cover, and set aside.

In the same skillet over medium heat, warm the remaining 1 Tbsp vegetable oil and melt the butter. Add the brussels sprouts and cook until browned, about 3 minutes. Flip and cook on the other side until browned, about 3 minutes more. Add the honey, vinegar, and a splash of water, stir, cover, and let simmer until the sprouts are tender, 2 to 3 minutes. Uncover and season with salt and pepper, then turn the heat to high, and continue to cook, 1 to 2 minutes, stirring occasionally, until the water evaporates and the sprouts are nicely browned on both sides. Turn off the heat and set aside.

TO MAKE THE SAUCE: In a small saucepan over medium heat, melt the butter. Add the plum jam and blueberries, mash the fruits with a fork, and cook until most of the liquid has evaporated and the sauce becomes thick, 10 to 15 minutes. Season with salt and stir in the honey, if desired.

Arrange the patties, brussels sprouts, and sauce on individual plates and serve immediately.

New Port Potato Pancakes

Due to our ship's unexpected detour to Spikeroog, my stay on Ard Skellig was shortened to a mere few days, just enough for the captain and crew to unload their cargo and stock provisions for the next leg of our journey. I spent my first day with the other travelers, lodged at the New Port, an inn where the air we breathed consisted wholly of the divine aroma of a large roast. Though ample of appetite and yearning for a taste of the roast, I opted for a lighter meal. I asked for the New Port's signature potato pancakes but—to the innkeep's surprise—with a side of sugar. My "unusual" request for a sweet sprinkling atop the crispy, golden pancakes elicited a tale of another recent visitor from the Continent—a witcher. He, too, had adored these scrumptious local favorites, but had insisted that sour cream was the sole acceptable topping. Later, satisfied with the fare but still hungry for tales, we encouraged the innkeep to tell us another. He shared one more—of the witcher's journey to the innkeep's ancestral island home of Undvik and of his encounter with the ice giant there . . .

MAKES 4 SERVINGS

1 lb 2 oz / 500g potatoes, peeled
1 tsp sour cream
Kosher salt
½ white onion
1 egg
2 Tbsp all-purpose flour
Vegetable oil for frying
Granulated sugar for serving (optional)
Sour cream for serving (optional)

In a medium bowl, using a box grater, finely grate two-thirds of the potatoes, then coarsely shred the remaining one-third. Add the sour cream and 2 pinches of salt, stir, cover, and set aside. After 5 minutes, carefully pour out the accumulated liquid into a separate small bowl. Transfer the grated potatoes to a fine-mesh sieve and set on top of the small bowl of the liquid. Using a spoon, gently press the potatoes to extract as much liquid as possible. Return the potatoes to the medium bowl. Cover both bowls and set aside. After 5 minutes, gently discard the water from the small bowl, leaving only the potato starch residue accumulated at the bottom.

In the bowl with the potato flesh, again using the smallest holes of the box grater, grate the onion. Add the potato starch from the second bowl, the egg, flour, and ½ tsp salt and stir until this batter is well combined.

Line a plate with a double layer of paper towels. Pour enough vegetable oil into a large nonstick skillet to cover the entire pan surface and set over medium heat. Check the temperature by adding a small dollop of batter to the pan; if it bubbles immediately, the oil is ready.

Using a large wooden spoon, scoop up a heaping 1 Tbsp of the batter and add to the pan, flattening it with the spoon to create a thin, oval pancake. Cook the pancake until it's golden brown, about 3 minutes on each side. Then transfer the pancake to the prepared plate and repeat with the remaining batter. Add more oil during frying, if needed.

Serve the pancakes hot, sprinkled with sugar, or alternatively with a dollop of sour cream.

Kaer Trolde
Ham and Apple Sandwiches

Kaer Trolde, a stronghold if I've ever seen one, simply towers over the port that lies below it. The keep is usually inaccessible to ordinary visitors. Yet, through a twist of fate, I arrived during a local celebration, a time when Ard Skelligers honor the founding of their clan and family seat. As legend has it, eons ago the hero Grymmdjarr carved the castle out of seaside rock with his bare hands. So as not to anger the gods, he refused hospitality to none, leaving the door of the feast hall open at all times for natives and foreigners alike. And so, in honor of the old tradition, the door stood open for me when I arrived. Inside the feast hall, the tables overflowed with mead, roasted meats, fish, and countless other fruits of the sea. Out of the corner of my eye, I spotted a sumptuous roast ham. Thin slices had been carved from it and set atop bread rolls. As I helped myself to a serving, topped with melted cheese, honey-caramelized apple, and a spicy horseradish sauce, I eavesdropped on a group of matrons, scolding their brood nearby. They told the story of a witch near Fornhala who taints cakes with spells. Greedy, sweet-toothed children who partake of the cakes turn into exceptionally shaggy bears for the rest of their days . . .

MAKES 2 SERVINGS

SPICY HORSERADISH SAUCE

⅓ cup / 80g mayonnaise

2 cornichons, minced

1 tsp prepared horseradish

½ tsp mustard

1 pinch kosher salt

1 pinch freshly ground black pepper

—

1 tsp unsalted butter

1 large tart apple, cored and thickly sliced

1 Tbsp floral honey

4 slices Cheddar cheese

2 whole-grain rolls

5½ oz / 160g Ard Skellig Roasted Ham (page 154) or store-bought ham, thinly sliced

In a small bowl, combine the mayonnaise, cornichons, horseradish, mustard, salt and pepper and stir to incorporate. Cover and set aside in the refrigerator for 30 minutes.

In a medium nonstick skillet over medium heat, melt the butter. Add the apple slices and cook until golden, about 2 minutes, then flip and cook for 1 minute more. Turn the heat to low, drizzle the slices with the honey, flip to coat, and let simmer until sticky, about 1 minute on each side. Turn off the heat, arrange the cheese on top of the warm apple slices, cover, and let sit until melted for 2 minutes.

Split the rolls in half, spread some of the sauce on each, and place sauce-side up on two plates. Evenly divide the cheesy caramelized apples and sliced ham among the rolls and then top with more sauce.

Serve the open-face sandwiches immediately.

Ard Skellig Roasted Ham

After savoring every morsel of my open-faced sandwich at Kaer Trolde, I was left wanting more. So I politely but insistently declined to leave the feast hall until someone agreed to betray to me the secret to roasting a ham to such succulence. Later, I managed to replicate the process in my own kitchen. The meat must first be marinated in local hard cider and spices, then boiled and coated with an aromatic glaze before being baked. The end result is a savory and juicy ham—delicious when served hot with gravy or when chilled and thinly sliced.

——◄ MAKES 8 SERVINGS ►——

SKELLIGE ISLES

3½ lb / 1.5kg fresh boneless ham shank
   or butt, preferably with fat cap
10 whole cloves

APPLE CIDER MARINADE
2 cups / 500ml hard cider, apple or pear
10 black peppercorns
2½ Tbsp kosher salt
2 bay leaves
2 allspice berries

HONEY-MUSTARD GLAZE
2 Tbsp floral honey
1 Tbsp vegetable oil
1 Tbsp dried marjoram
2 tsp spicy mustard
1 tsp kosher salt
2 pinches freshly ground black pepper

———◇———

If the pork is not round, compact it into a tight ball and tie it into a roast shape with kitchen twine. Stick the cloves into the top of the meat, leaving their tops visible.

TO MAKE THE MARINADE: In a large bowl, combine the cider, peppercorns, salt, bay leaves, and allspice berries and stir to incorporate.

Place the pork in the marinade, add enough cold water to cover entirely, cover the bowl with a lid, and refrigerate for 24 hours. Turn over the pork every 6 hours so it can marinate evenly.

Remove the pork from the fridge about 1 hour before cooking to take the chill off.

Pour all the marinade into a large saucepan over high heat and bring to a boil. Place the pork in the pan and parboil for 2 minutes, turning once. Add more water to cover the meat entirely, cover the pan with a lid, then turn the heat to low and let simmer until the meat is knife-tender, about 120 minutes. If the meat still feels tough when you pierce it with the tip of a knife, continue to cook, then drain and tightly wrap in aluminum foil. Set aside for 30 minutes.

TO MAKE THE GLAZE: While the meat is cooking, in a small bowl, combine the honey, vegetable oil, marjoram, mustard, salt, and pepper and stir to incorporate. Set aside.

Preheat the oven to 425°F / 220°C.

When ready to roast, unwrap the pork. If it has a fat cap, using a sharp knife, slightly score a crisscross pattern. Place the pork in a small roasting pan and brush the surface evenly with the glaze.

Roast the pork, uncovered, until the top is heavily browned, about 20 minutes.

Remove the pork from the oven and let it rest for 20 minutes before slicing and serving.

Rannvaig Pork
in Onion and Cheese Gravy with Groats

Though the island's icy winds discouraged leisurely strolls, I refused to remain idle in the comfort of the inn. Making full use of my last day on Ard Skellig, I ventured to the fishing village of Rannvaig with a few of my fellow travelers. My choice of Rannvaig as a destination was no accident. I had heard of horse races run in this village to honor the goddess Freya. Dubbed the Heroes' Pursuits, the races are as highly hazardous as they are respected by local folk. Mountain brooks babbled, the sun shone bright and frosted heather twinkled as I followed a rocky path to a place marked off with pennants flapping in the wind. The air was thick with competitive energy, all gathered were abuzz. To my surprise, the breeze also carried the tantalizing aroma of a rich stew, simmering in a cauldron nearby. Learning that the simple yet hearty dish had been made for race participants and spectators alike, I claimed my bowl without delay. Roasted buckwheat, tender meat, and onion, beneath a thick smothering of mustard-cheese sauce . . . By the gods . . . With my belly full and my body warmed, the festive fervor took hold of me, too. I eagerly followed the crowd gathering at the village's edge to observe the race participants make their final preparations.

MAKES 2 TO 4 SERVINGS

2 Tbsp vegetable oil or lard

3 medium onions, sliced

Kosher salt

2 garlic cloves, peeled and minced

1 cup / 240ml vegetable stock or water

12 oz / 340g boneless pork shoulder or loin

Freshly ground black pepper

2 tsp spicy mustard

1 tsp dried savory

1 tsp dried parsley flakes

¾ cup / 140g roasted buckwheat groats

1⅓ cups / 320ml water

¼ cup / 60ml heavy cream

1 tsp all-purpose flour

½ cup / 50g cheese (such as Gouda or Cheddar), shredded

In a medium nonstick skillet over medium-high heat, warm 1 Tbsp of the vegetable oil. Add the onion and a pinch of salt and cook, stirring frequently, until lightly browned, about 5 minutes. Add the garlic and stir-fry for 30 seconds. Transfer the contents of the skillet to a medium saucepan over low heat, add the vegetable stock, and bring to a simmer.

Place the pork on a cutting board, cut into chunks, gently flatten with a meat mallet, and lightly sprinkle with salt and pepper.

Recipe continues

In the same skillet over medium-high heat, warm the remaining 1 Tbsp vegetable oil. Add the pork and cook until lightly browned, about 2 minutes, then flip and continue to cook for 1 minute more. Transfer the meat to the pan with the onion. Add a splash of water to the skillet, deglaze, scraping up the browned bits with a wooden spoon, and add to the saucepan.

Add the mustard, savory, and parsley to the saucepan and stir. Turn the heat to low, cover, and let simmer, stirring occasionally, until the meat is tender, about 40 minutes.

While the meat is cooking, put the buckwheat groats in a fine-mesh sieve, rinse with cold water, and then transfer to a medium saucepan over high heat. Add the water and

¾ tsp salt, cover, and bring to a boil. Then turn the heat to low and cook, without stirring, for 15 minutes. Turn off the heat, stir, cover, and set aside for 2 minutes, until the groats are soft (they should soak up all the water).

In a small bowl, whisk the cream and flour together. Gradually add the cream mixture to the saucepan with the pork, stirring constantly. Season with salt and pepper, stir to incorporate, and let simmer until the gravy becomes thick, a couple of minutes. Then gradually add the cheese and gently stir until the cheese is fully melted. Turn off the heat.

Serve the groats in individual bowls along with a generous portion of the gravy.

Faroe Herring in Oil
with Cranberries and Onions

A settlement on the archipelago's southernmost isle, Faroe, was the final stop on my tour of Skellige. Though many of my fellow travelers decided to remain on board, I chose to visit Harviken and peek inside the island's sole tavern, a quaint spot tucked between two homesteads. As I walked past a group of apparent regulars, I glanced at the fare before them. The tavernkeep insisted I try a dish that would be "safe for an outsider's gut," yet I had already set my eyes on a prize. In the end, I sat down with a plate of hard-fought herring in oil. Cranberries, pickled onions, colored peppercorns, and dill rounded off the dish nicely. Served with hearty bread to wipe up any remaining oil, this outsider left no flavor to waste.

MAKES 6 SERVINGS

6 small brined herring fillets
1 small red onion, sliced
3 Tbsp distilled white vinegar or apple cider vinegar
¼ cup / 35g dried cranberries
4 sprigs dill
15 mixed peppercorns
1 cup / 240ml sunflower oil or canola oil, or as needed
Rustic bread for serving

In a medium bowl, combine the herring and water to cover and let soak for about 2 hours to get rid of the excess salt (repeat the step with fresh water if needed), and then drain and pat dry with paper towels. You can use the fillets whole or cut them into 1½ inch / 4cm slices.

While the herring is soaking, in a small bowl, combine the onion and vinegar and let sit for 30 minutes, and then drain.

In another small bowl, combine the cranberries with warm water to cover, and let soak for 15 minutes, and then drain.

In a medium airtight container or in a 32-ounce jar with a lid, arrange the ingredients in layers, starting with the marinated onion slices, then adding a sprig of dill, a few cranberries and peppercorns, and finally the herring. Repeat until you run out of ingredients and then top with the sunflower oil so all ingredients are well submerged.

Cover and refrigerate for 2 to 3 days before serving to allow the flavors to develop. Serve the herring with hunks of rustic bread.

Store, covered, in the fridge for up to 5 days.

Harviken Dried-Fruit Brew

My Faroe herring came with a mug of spiced compote brewed from dried and smoked fruits. This particular assortment added both sweet and tart notes that paired wonderfully with warmed spices. Needless to say, I could not stop at one cup. After a few hours, I left Harviken with a new culinary experience and a small memento—a colorful, handwoven sash. And I began to wonder . . . was this my farewell to Skellige and its crisp island air? No. I vowed to return. I would have to. Else how could I look forward to the next phase of my journey with clear eyes and an open mind? So, oath made, I boarded our ship, eager to set sail for Toussaint and leave the wild beauty of the Skellige Isles behind. For a time.

MAKES 1½ QUARTS / 1.5L

DRIED FRUIT MIX
3 oz / 80g dried pears or smoked dried pears
2½ oz / 70g dried apricots
2½ oz / 70g dried plums (pitted prunes)
1 oz / 30g dried smoked plums (optional)
1¾ oz / 50g dried cranberries
1¾ oz / 50g dried apple slices
—
1½ qt / 1.5L water
4 whole cloves
1 cinnamon stick
Floral honey for sweetening (optional)
2 Tbsp apple cider vinegar (optional)

TO MAKE THE FRUIT MIX: In a small bowl, combine all the dried fruits and rinse with cold water.

In a medium saucepan, combine the water, cloves, cinnamon stick, and dried fruit mix. Cover and let soak for 3 hours.

Set the saucepan, uncovered, over medium heat and bring the mixture to a boil. Then turn the heat to low and let simmer, stirring occasionally, for 20 minutes. Turn off the heat, cover, and let sit for 1 hour. For a sweeter drink, stir in the honey; for a more refreshing taste, stir in the vinegar.

You can enjoy the drink with the cooked fruits (remove the cloves and cinnamon stick) or strain beforehand. Serve slightly warm or chilled.

NOTES
In addition to serving this as a drink, you can strain the liquid (remove the cloves and cinnamon stick), and serve the cooked fruits as a standalone dessert, topped with whipped cream. Or use the fruit as a topping for Ciri's Breakfast Porridge (page 233).

If you can find smoked dried pears or smoked dried plums, use them here, but be careful with smoked fruits—their taste can be quite strong, so use sparingly and start with smaller quantities.

BEAUCLAIR

There is but one place on all the Continent where scorching days always turn to sultry nights, where, come evening, the air smells of fine wine, rose blossoms and succulent fare prepared in tavern cellars. Beauclair is the shining capital and beating heart of Toussaint, a land lying in the shadow of snow-capped Mount Gorgon, a land of fairy tales made real. An idyllic enclave for common folk, nobility and palace visitors alike, it is where drink and dance flow seemingly without end. Each day, Beauclair's vibrant alleyways and sun-drenched boulevards become crowded with merchants, travelers and winery proprietors. The latter supply their sanguine nectars to culinary experts at local taverns like the Adder and Jewels Winery or the Pheasantry. The Toussantois serve wine alongside all meals, in ornamental chalices, of course, but also use it as an ingredient in many of the duchy's traditional dishes. The region's cuisine is, quite simply, artistry on a fork. Even specialties enjoyed mostly by the common rabble are treasured and desired by the duchy's nobility and wellborn. And, as I expected, revels within the city walls grow to new heights of lavishness as holidays approach, be it *Yule*, *Belleteyn* or, perhaps most importantly, the Festival of the Vat. On these special occasions, Beauclair's main square transforms into a bustling jubilee, lit with lanterns and lined with rose-garlanded tents, where one can savor the finest wines and refreshments and the many other tempting delights Beauclair has to offer.

Étoile Blanche Pasta at the Adder and Jewels Winery

Soon after arriving in Beauclair, I presented myself at the palace so as to begin work on a cartographic project commissioned by the ducal court. In preparation for it, I first consulted its scope and purpose with the court chamberlain, then made frequent visits to the renowned Beauclair Library. While at the library, with the court librarian's aid, I familiarized myself with its vast collection of maps. My aim was to draft the most accurate representation of the Continent to date. While consulting with the chamberlain, I was surprised to hear that my pace of work and apparent academic fervor might prove a disruption to the palace's serene air. "'Work doth one ennoble,'" he said, "'while sloth doth one gratify'—a local mantra, if you will. And for us Beauclarois, gratification is sacred!" Thus, while continuing to make visible progress in my map-making, I allowed myself ample moments of sloth as well. Come my first evening free of toil, I embarked on an exploration of the local cuisine at one of the city's many taverns—The Adder and Jewels. Affiliated with a winery, the establishment was housed in a townhouse cellar and came highly recommended by courtiers and palace servants alike. The wine list was impressive, while the dishes based on the recipes of the legendary elven chef Ra'mses Gor-Thon proved more than a match. Gor-Thon's once-lost culinary legacy had been rediscovered years before. The tavernkeep who came into possession of his records had incorporated the chef-of-yore's last surviving recipes into the menu. As I pored over it, I found myself torn between the Étoile Blanche Pasta and a crayfish boil. In the end, my passion for noodles proved decisive. The wide ribbons were served with a range of tasty additions—fried turkey marinated in exotic spices and yogurt, aromatic chanterelles, sweet tomatoes, a handful of arugula, and a creamy ricotta cheese. Paired with a red wine from the Pomerol Vineyard, it proved the very gratification I had set out to find.

— MAKES 2 SERVINGS —

CURRY SPICE MARINADE
2 Tbsp plain Greek yogurt
2 garlic cloves, minced
1 tsp Ofieri Spice Blend (page 118) or curry powder
¾ tsp kosher salt
—
1 to 2 boneless, skinless turkey or chicken breasts (about 9 oz / 250g)
3½ oz / 100g chanterelle or button mushrooms

1 Tbsp unsalted butter
Kosher salt and freshly ground black pepper
3 Tbsp extra-virgin olive oil
¼ cup / 60ml semidry red wine
7 oz / 200g fresh egg pasta (such as tagliatelle)
10 cherry tomatoes, halved
½ cup / 100g ricotta cheese, at room temperature
Arugula for garnishing

Recipe continues

TO MAKE THE MARINADE: In a small bowl, combine the yogurt, garlic, spice blend, and salt and stir to incorporate.

Add the turkey to the marinade and turn to coat, then place the bowl in the refrigerator for 1 hour. About 20 minutes before you're ready to cook, remove the meat from the fridge, shake off excess marinade into the bowl, then set on a plate and discard the marinade.

Bring a kettle of water to a boil.

If using chanterelles, clean the sand residue with a brush, then transfer to a bowl, add 1 teaspoon salt, and cover with boiling water. Stir and let sit for 1 minute, then use a slotted spoon to remove the mushrooms, and discard the water with the sand residue. Pat the mushrooms dry with a paper towel and cut larger ones into chunks of similar size. If using button mushrooms, clean and slice thinly.

In a medium nonstick skillet over medium heat, melt the butter. Add the mushrooms and cook undisturbed for 2 to 3 minutes, then stir once or twice and continue to cook until lightly browned and just tender, about 5 minutes more. Season with salt and pepper, transfer to a plate, cover, and set aside.

In the same skillet over medium-high heat, warm 1 Tbsp of the olive oil. Add the marinated turkey and cook for about 3 minutes on each side, until golden brown. Turn the heat to medium, add the wine, flipping the meat once or twice to coat, then cover and cook for another 2 minutes. Uncover, flip to coat once more, and cook until liquid evaporates. Turn off the heat, transfer the meat to a cutting board, and let rest for about 5 minutes. Cut the meat across the grain into ⅛-inch / 3mm strips.

Bring a large saucepan of water to a boil over high heat. Add 1 Tbsp salt and the pasta and cook, stirring occasionally, until al dente according to the package directions. Drain but don't rinse.

In the same skillet over high heat, warm the remaining 2 Tbsp olive oil. Add the tomatoes, cut-side down, and cook for about 1 minute. Then add the cooked pasta, mushrooms, and meat strips and stir-fry for about 1 minute more to evenly combine the ingredients. Transfer to a large serving plate.

Using a teaspoon, arrange dollops of the ricotta cheese on top of the pasta and garnish with arugula leaves. Sprinkle with pepper and serve immediately.

Beauclair Sangria

My meal consumed with satisfaction, I resolved to last out the evening at the Adder and Jewels. I felt it would be in poor taste—disrespectful, even— not to sample more of the expertly assembled wine list to which the establishment owed its fame. Also, the mere varieties, vintages, and barrels on display around the dining room did wonders to arouse my curiosity. I opted to taste the Saint Mathieu rouge, the Sansretour pinot noir, and the Sansretour chardonnay among others, complemented by a platter of local cheeses and grapes. Yet amongst all the flavor profiles I sampled, I crowned the sangria as queen cup of the evening. It is made using a unique blend of red wine, spices and sun-ripened fruit, including raspberries, blueberries, strawberries, and citruses, all of local provenance. Though most folk enjoy it as a cool refreshment on sweltering days, the barmaid explained, this fact need not mean the sangria loses its appeal come nightfall. Bottles came and went. I only noticed the time that had passed when the tavernkeep announced last call and I realized nearly all other patrons had long departed. Belly full and soul satisfied, I set out for the palace. I felt profoundly confident, at ease in my new surroundings, as if the sangria had given me almost limitless courage. Had the ghost of a headless knight errant appeared before me, I might well have asked him for a ride. Unfortunately, contrary to common belief, I've found that knights—spectral or otherwise—rarely appear when most needed. So I passed through the slumbering city, through the market square, and across the bridge between Old Town and the palace, the scent of blooming roses my sole companion . . .

MAKES 6 CUPS / 1.4L

---

3 cups / 720ml dry red wine

1 cup / 240ml 100% apple juice

½ cup 100% cranberry juice

1½ cups / 150g mixed fresh or frozen fruits (such as raspberries, blueberries, and halved strawberries)

1 lemon, thinly sliced

1 orange, thinly sliced

1 cinnamon stick

3 whole cloves

1 star anise pod (optional)

1 to 2 Tbsp floral honey

½ cup / 120ml sparkling water (optional)

In a large bowl or pitcher, combine the wine, apple juice, cranberry juice, mixed fruits, lemon, orange, cinnamon stick, cloves, and star anise (if using). Stir and refrigerate, covered, for at least 1 hour or, for better flavor, up to 6 hours. Taste and sweeten with the honey and add the sparkling water, if desired.

Pour the chilled drink, including chunks of fruit, into punch glasses and serve.

The Gran'place Festival Honey Croissants

Beautiful weather, scrumptious food and wine, seemingly nonstop entertainment—thus passes a typical day in Beauclair. Each day, in fact, seems a swift flow of revelry. Consequently, keeping up oft seems a challenge. Needless to say, I was not at all surprised to see the city's largest marketplace abustle, final preparations for a festival underway. A herald, voice clear and booming, announced the start of a spectacle—a play to be staged in the ruins of the Seidhe Llygad Amphitheatre. It was rumored a theater troupe had sought to perform a controversial work with a vampire motif. Yet at the behest of the ducal court, the Imperial Academy of Drama had stepped in with a staging of *A Midsummer Night's Daydream*. Market stalls usually used by local artists to sell their paintings promptly disappeared from the square. They were replaced with tables and with crates filled with Vis la Crac wine. While I strolled through the milling crowd, restless with anticipation, I came across a small confectionary stand, the proprietor inviting passersby to sample his fare. Given the commotion of the festival, he explained, he had pared down his offerings to a simplified take on his popular honey croissants with plum filling. Yet, the baker assured me, these were of no lesser quality. I left the busy Gran'place Market, croissants in hand, and found a quiet nook on a side street. There, I put his claims to the test. Indeed, in the mild sweetness, buttery flakes, and delicate crispiness, I found absolutely no flaw.

MAKES 8 CROISSANTS

1 tsp instant yeast, or 10g fresh yeast, crumbled
½ cup / 120ml whole milk, with more for brushing
2 tbsp vegetable oil
4 Tbsp floral honey, plus 3 Tbsp for glazing
1 cup / 120g sifted all-purpose flour,
   with more for sprinkling
½ cup / 55g sifted whole-wheat flour
½ tsp kosher salt
½ tsp grated lemon zest (optional)
½ cup / 110g unsalted butter at room temperature
4 tsp plum jam

In a large bowl, combine the yeast, milk, oil, and 4 Tbsp of the honey and whisk until the yeast is dissolved.

Add both flours, salt, and lemon zest (if using) and give it a brief stir with a fork.

Lightly flour a work surface. Transfer the dough to the prepared surface and knead briefly until just smooth. Form the dough into a ball, transfer to a bowl, cover with a clean kitchen towel, and let the dough rise in a warm place until doubled in size, 1½ to 2 hours.

Recipe continues

Lightly sprinkle the work surface with flour. Divide the dough into two equal portions and, using a rolling pin, roll out each to a 6 by 16-inch / 15 by 40cm rectangle. Evenly spread the softened butter on one rectangle, stopping ⅕ inch / 0.5cm from each edge. Cover with the second rectangle, aligning all the edges, and gently press down with the palm of your hand to seal the layers together. With a long side facing you, fold the left side of the layered dough into the center, fold the right side of the dough into the center, and then fold in half. Gently press the surface of the dough with your palm to seal the layers together.

Wrap the dough with parchment paper and refrigerate for 45 minutes. Remove the dough from the fridge, roll out into a 6 by 16-inch / 15 by 40cm rectangle, repeat the folding process once more, wrap in parchment paper and refrigerate for 30 minutes.

Line a baking sheet with parchment paper.

Remove the dough from the fridge and roll out again into a 7 by 16-inch / 18 by 40cm rectangle that is ⅕ inch / 5mm thick. If the dough is too sticky while rolling, sprinkle with additional all-purpose flour.

Mark one long side of the dough into five 3-inch / 8cm lengths. On the other long side of the dough, start at 4cm from one side and mark four 3-inch / 8cm lengths. Using a sharp knife, alternating from one side to the other, cut out eight triangles.

Place ½ tsp of the plum jam about ½ inch / 1.5cm from the wider edge of each triangle. Pull the tip and stretch the wider end slightly. Working from the wider edge, gently roll the dough, slightly bending the left and right sides into a crescent shape. Arrange the croissants on the prepared baking sheet about 2 inches / 5cm apart, cover with a kitchen towel, and let rise at room temperature until doubled in size, about 1½ hours.

Preheat the oven to 400°F / 200°C.

Brush the top of the croissants with milk. Bake the croissants until golden brown, 15 to 20 minutes. Remove from the oven and transfer to a wire rack to cool for about 5 minutes. Then, using a brush, spread the remaining 3 Tbsp honey on the tops and let them cool slightly before serving.

Chocolate Soufflé
with Sangreal Red Wine Sauce

As the sun began slowly to set, I put aside my work tools and turned my attention to an envelope holding an official invitation from Louis, the ducal family's chef in Beauclair and a splendid man to boot. For having recognized my interest in the culinary arts, he had not only secured an invitation for me to attend the ducal festivities, but had asked me to assist in preparing the dish that would represent the ducal kitchen. Once I reached our appointed meeting spot and found Louis amidst the crowd and tents, he quickly opened my eyes to the secrets of many dishes brought that day to Beauclair from all corners of Toussaint. For the occasion, the ducal kitchen aimed to demonstrate its expertise by resurrecting an old recipe. This was for a silky chocolate confection, once the favorite dessert of Ademarta, the first Lady of Beauclair. Achieving the proper consistency for the soufflé, even aided by this culinary virtuoso, required a steady hand and extraordinary attention to detail. Yet the effort was worth it. The chocolatey, fluffy richness paired with the tangy sweetness of a blood-red Sangreal wine sauce attested boldly to Beauclair's madly rich culinary traditions. Simply put, 'twas an experience I shall not soon forget . . .

——— ◄ MAKES 2 SMALL SOUFFLÉS ► ———

RED WINE SAUCE
¾ cup / 175ml dry red wine (such as Bordeaux)
1½ Tbsp granulated sugar
1½ Tbsp floral honey
1 pinch Zerrikanian Spice Blend (page 42; optional) or cinnamon

SOUFFLÉS
5 Tbsp / 70ml heavy cream
3½ oz / 100g dark chocolate (70% cocoa), chopped
Unsalted butter, at room temperature, for greasing
2 Tbsp superfine sugar, with more for sprinkling
2 eggs, separated
Kosher salt
2 drops lemon juice

TO MAKE THE SAUCE: In a small saucepan over medium heat, combine the wine and granulated sugar and bring to a boil. Turn the heat to low and let simmer, uncovered, until the sauce thickens and is reduced to ¼ cup / 60ml, 10 to 15 minutes. Turn off the heat, add the honey, and season with the spice blend (if using), then stir to combine and set aside to cool to room temperature.

TO MAKE THE SOUFFLÉS: In a small saucepan over medium-high heat, bring the cream to a boil. Turn off the heat, add the chocolate, and stir until the chocolate is fully melted. Set aside to cool to lukewarm.

Preheat the oven to 400°F / 200°C. Grease two 5 oz / 140ml ramekins with butter and sprinkle the bottoms with superfine sugar. Shake out any excess sugar.

Recipe continues

Add the egg yolks to the lukewarm mixture and stir vigorously to combine.

In a metal bowl, combine the egg whites and a pinch of salt and, using a whisk, whip until foamy. Continue whisking into soft peaks, then gradually add the super-fine sugar. Once the whites are fully whipped, gently fold in the lemon juice.

Add one-third of the whipped whites to the cream-chocolate mixture and gently stir to incorporate. Then, using a spatula, gently fold in the remaining two-thirds of the whites; take care not to overmix this batter.

Pour the chocolate batter into the prepared ramekins and, using a knife or a spatula, smooth out the tops. Run your thumb around the inside edge of each ramekin to create a gap between the batter and the sides of the ramekins.

Place the ramekins in the oven and, after 1 minute, lower the oven temperature to 350°F / 185°C. Continue to bake until the soufflés have risen significantly, 11 to 13 minutes. Remove from the oven (the soufflés will slightly deflate).

Serve the soufflés immediately with a generous portion of the wine sauce.

The Pheasantry's Beef Stew

During my sojourn in Beauclair, I came to learn a rather important travelers' truth—one day with a guide is worth a hundred without. While working in the palace library, I was fortunate enough to meet a group of future architects, all Beauclair natives. They became my guides and dining companions, introducing me to some of the best eateries tucked away in the city's nooks and corners. And so it happened that my boisterous new comrades, enthusiasts of the famed architect Faramond, led me to the Pheasantry—a culinary and cultural experience *de rigueur*. I encouraged them to draw on their local wisdom and choose for me a dish that, to their minds, would capture the tavern's spirit. So I promptly sampled the Pheasantry's exquisitely aromatic beef stew—simmered with sautéed mushrooms, carrots, and onions, and further enriched with plums, the inn's secret ingredient. Served with a creamy potato purée, the stew proved worthy of its reputation and more. After the meal, my comrades and I moved to a table on the terrace, taking our as yet unemptied bottles of wine with us. There, we witnessed the exciting conclusion of the Great Beauclair Gwent Tournament. Truth be told, I was disappointed to see the grand finale of this tourney of wits turn into a crude brawl. Yet, as my companions casually noted, I had at least experienced Toussaint's "true culture" firsthand.

MAKES 4 SERVINGS

5 oz / 150g slab bacon, cubed

1¼ lb / 570g beef chuck, cut into 1½-inch / 4cm chunks

Kosher salt

All-purpose flour for coating

1½ cups / 360ml dry red wine, or as needed

2 Tbsp vegetable oil

1 large onion, diced

2 celery stalks, diced

2 garlic cloves, smashed and peeled

2 cups / 480ml beef stock or water

1 bunch flat-leaf parsley (tied in a bundle), plus chopped leaves for garnish

2 bay leaves

3 sprigs thyme, or 1 tsp dried

5 dried plums (pitted prunes), finely chopped

1 large carrot, thickly sliced

9 oz / 250g button mushrooms (halved if large)

2 Tbsp unsalted butter

Freshly ground black pepper

3½ oz / 100g shallots, quartered

MASHED POTATOES

2 medium potatoes, peeled

Kosher salt

1 Tbsp unsalted butter

2 Tbsp Parmesan, grated

1 pinch nutmeg

Fresh baguette for serving (optional)

In a medium nonstick skillet over medium heat, combine the bacon and a splash of water and cook, stirring occasionally, until the water evaporates, then fry until browned, about 5 minutes more. Transfer the bacon to a large saucepan or Dutch oven but set aside the skillet with the bacon fat.

Recipe continues

Sprinkle the beef with salt. Place some flour in a small bowl and add the beef, tossing to coat. Then shake off the excess.

Set the same skillet with the bacon fat over medium-high heat, add the beef in batches, without overcrowding the pan so the chunks don't stick together, and cook until browned, about 1 minute on each side. Do not stir; just flip the chunks on each side to brown evenly. As the beef finishes cooking, transfer to the saucepan with the bacon, add the wine, set over low heat, and bring to a simmer.

In the same skillet over medium heat, warm 1 Tbsp of the vegetable oil. Add the onion and celery and cook, stirring frequently, until lightly browned, about 4 minutes. Then add the garlic and stir-fry for about 30 seconds more. Transfer everything to the pan with the bacon and beef. Add a splash of wine to the skillet and deglaze, scraping up the browned bits with a wooden spoon, then add the liquid to the saucepan.

Add the beef stock, parsley, bay leaves, thyme, and plums to the saucepan, stir, cover, and let simmer. After 30 minutes, remove the parsley and thyme sprigs. Continue to simmer, stirring occasionally.

While the meat is cooking, in the same skillet over medium heat, warm the remaining 1 Tbsp vegetable oil. Add the carrot and cook until golden brown on both sides, about 4 minutes. Transfer to a medium bowl, cover, and set aside.

Rinse the mushrooms with cold water and pat dry. In the same skillet over medium heat, melt 1 Tbsp of the butter. Add the mushrooms and cook, stirring once or twice, until golden brown, 3 to 4 minutes. Season with salt and pepper, and then transfer to the bowl with the carrots and set aside.

In the same skillet over medium heat, warm the remaining 1 Tbsp butter. Add the shallot and cook, stirring occasionally, until lightly browned, about 4 minutes. Add the shallot to the bowl with the carrot and mushrooms.

After the meat has simmered for about 1½ hours, discard the bay leaves and add the mushrooms, onion, and carrot. Continue to simmer, adding a splash more wine if needed, until the meat is tender and the stew is thick, about 30 minutes more. At the very end, season with salt and pepper. The stew can be served right away or refrigerated overnight to let the flavors develop; reheat gently over low heat.

TO MAKE THE MASHED POTATOES: In a medium saucepan, add potatoes and enough water to cover. Add 1 tsp salt and cook over medium heat until tender, about 30 minutes. Drain the potatoes and let sit for 5 minutes. Using a masher or fork, mash the potatoes. Add the butter and stir until well combined, then stir in the cheese and nutmeg.

Divide the mashed potatoes among individual bowls, top with the stew, and garnish with parsley. Serve immediately with hunks of fresh baguette, if desired.

Pear and Est Est Wine Tart

Another encounter with Beauclairois cuisine awaited me during the New Wine Festival, a joyous occasion that features samplings of the current year's vintage from many wineries. The revelries included a scavenger hunt spanning the palace gardens, the city, and its surroundings. The game's participants set out in search of objects constituting clues to tasks they were then to perform. Thus, on that day, I could be seen emerging from a hedge bush—hair tousled, tunic rumpled—proudly presenting a pheasant feather I had been tasked with finding. Accomplishing the feat meant I could attempt the next. Following the clue attached to the feather, I reached a bakery in Lolivier Square. There, another challenge awaited: to bake a pear tart per a provided recipe. This task helped me recover some of the enthusiasm I had lost while crawling through the hedges. As I kneaded the ground almonds into my pastry dough, I nibbled on pears coated in a caramel sauce made with exquisite Est Est white wine and Zerrikanian spices. First attempt though it was, I managed to produce a perfect tart. The evaluating confectioner praised it highly, ensuring that I passed to the game's next stage. And though I was not crowned the ultimate victor that day, as I jotted down the tart recipe from memory, I knew I had walked away with the ultimate prize.

⟥——————⟤ MAKES 6 SERVINGS ⟥——————⟤

CRUST
¾ cup / 90g sifted all-purpose flour
¼ cup / 30g almonds, ground or finely chopped
2 Tbsp granulated sugar
¼ cup / 60g unsalted butter, cold, diced
3 Tbsp sour cream

FILLING
1 lb / 450g pears, peeled, halved, and cored
¾ cup / 180ml white wine, with more for brushing
½ cup / 100g granulated sugar
2 Tbsp unsalted butter
Kosher salt
1 pinch ground cloves
1 star anise pod (optional)
—
Crème fraîche, ice cream, or whipped cream for serving

TO MAKE THE CRUST: In a medium bowl, using your fingers or a pastry blender, rub together the flour, almonds, sugar, and butter until the mixture is the consistency of coarse bread crumbs. Add the sour cream and knead briefly, just until combined. In the bowl, form the dough into a flat disk, cover with a kitchen towel, and refrigerate for 30 minutes.

TO MAKE THE FILLING: Place the pears on a large plate, brush with white wine, cover with aluminum foil or plastic wrap, and set aside.

Recipe continues

In a large nonstick skillet over medium-high heat, combine the sugar and the wine and cook, stirring occasionally, until the sugar dissolves and the mixture turns amber, about 15 minutes. Turn the heat to low, add the butter and a pinch of salt, and let simmer, stirring vigorously, until the caramel sauce becomes thick, about 2 minutes. Add the pears and cloves and let simmer, gently flipping them a few times, until the pears are just tender, about 10 minutes. Using a spatula, gently transfer the pears to a shallow 8-inch / 20cm round baking dish or cake pan, arranging them, cored-side down and pointed ends toward the center, next to each other around the edge of the dish. Continue to cook the sauce until it is the thickness of honey, 5 to 10 minutes more.

Pour the caramel sauce over the pears. Place the star anise (if using) in the center of the pan and set aside to cool.

Preheat the oven to 400°F / 200°C.

While the pears are cooling, remove the dough from the fridge and let it sit at room temperature for 10 minutes to take the chill off. Lightly flour a work surface and, using a rolling pin, roll out the dough into a 12-inch / 30cm circle about 1/16 inch / 2mm thick. Carefully place the rolled dough on top of the pears and, using your hands, gently tuck the dough around the fruit, keeping the pear halves together, and then slightly fold the edges inward.

Bake the tart until the crust is nicely browned on the top, about 40 minutes. Remove from the oven and let cool at room temperature for about 30 minutes. Run a knife around the outside edges of the crust, then place a flat plate upside down on top and, holding firmly, quickly flip to the other side.

Slice the tart into wedges and serve with crème fraîche, ice cream, or whipped cream.

VARIATION: To get a slightly different flavor profile for the caramel sauce, use red wine instead of white. This will also turn the sauce blood red.

Duchess's Duck Confit

Louis, the palace chef whom I had befriended, was kind enough to invite me to his home. There, he treated me to many more traditional Beauclairois dishes in an informal, domestic rather than stiff courtly setting. As you might imagine, I spent most of my time in his kitchen, the air thick with the aroma of fresh herbs. Much like in my own home in Kovir, his kitchen was the favored meeting place for members of his household. His family taught me about new ingredients and recipes, and we spent much time debating the merits of using precise measurements as opposed to following one's instincts and cooking with dollops and dashes, splashes and handfuls. Naturally, I lent a hand where I could, better to penetrate the secrets of their family recipes. It was there that I learned to prepare duck confit—a dish that takes time but rewards handsomely those with some patience. Duck legs—rubbed with salt, pepper, and herbs—must be cooked slowly in oil with garlic and rosemary. The result is a perfectly seasoned, delicate, melt-in-the-mouth meat—each bite so delightful as to make it irresistible to cooks. So much so, in fact, the duck outright fails to reach the dinner table at times . . .

MAKES 4 SERVINGS

2¼ tsp kosher salt
1¼ tsp dried savory
1¼ tsp dried marjoram
¾ tsp freshly ground black pepper
4 duck legs (about 8 oz / 225g each)
4 garlic cloves, lightly crushed
2 bay leaves
2 small sprigs rosemary
About 6 cups / 1.4L vegetable oil or duck lard
   (melted and cooled to lukewarm)

In a small bowl, combine the salt, savory, marjoram, and pepper. Rub this spice mix over all of the surfaces of the duck legs.

Arrange the duck legs in a 13 by 9-inch / 33 by 23cm baking dish, skin-side up, and refrigerate, uncovered, for 24 hours.

About 1 hour before baking, remove the duck legs from the fridge and pat dry with paper towels. Add the garlic, bay leaves, and rosemary and pour in the cooking fat so that the meat is fully submerged. Cover with a lid or aluminum foil. Carefully transfer the dish to the oven and turn the temperature to 250°F / 120°C.

Bake the duck until the meat is tender and pulls off the end of the drumstick, about 4 hours. (The skin on the legs will still be pale.) Remove the dish from the oven, discard the bay leaves and rosemary, and let cool to lukewarm. Pour the cooking liquid into a separate container and let cool completely. Scoop the fat that has accumulated on top and set aside; discard the liquid.

At this point, you can brown the duck and serve, or store it to serve later (the flavor will continue to develop while stored). To store, submerge the duck completely in the reserved cooking fat and refrigerate for 3 days (or up to 1 month).

Before serving, arrange the legs skin-side up in a baking dish (scraping off any excess fat if the duck has been stored in the fridge) and bake in a 400°F / 200°C oven until the skin is nicely browned, 15 to 20 minutes.

Midinváerne Honey Spice Cake

One day, after quickly concluding my business at the flea market in Epona Square, I made for the Pheasantry, which was due to celebrate the anniversary of its founding. To mark the occasion, the tavern displayed a series of artifacts from its history. The menu, too, had been adjusted to include classic dishes upon which the establishment had built its reputation. Among these was their ever-popular gingerbread, based on the recipe of legendary elven chef Ra'mses Gor-Thon, for which a spot is always made on Beauclairois tables during the observance of *Midinváerne*. While waiting to collect my own gingerbread, I studied the original written recipe, on display inside a glass case, as well as the famous spoon key to the door of the legendary chef's workshop. The Pheasantry had drawn a crowd that day. I acquired two gingerbread loaves and took a smaller piece on a tasting plate to eat on the terrace under the Toussaint sun. As I sat, having my cake and eating it, too, I began reading a book of fairy tales I had procured at the market earlier that day. It was titled *Tales of the Merchant of Mirrors*. How amusing and appropriate, I thought, that the book provided such interesting perspectives on time as a culinary concept. For time is a crucial ingredient, giving gingerbread the right consistency, conjuring the ideal crunch of the outer crust and the delicious moistness within.

MAKES 10 SERVINGS

2 Tbsp whole milk

⅔ cup / 220g floral honey

⅓ cup / 110g buckwheat honey

7 Tbsp / 100g unsalted butter

1 egg

1⅓ cups / 170g spelt flour, or ⅔ cup / 90g all-purpose flour plus ⅔ cup / 80g whole-wheat flour

3½ tsp Zerrikanian Spice Blend (page 42) or 4 tsp gingerbread spice

Kosher salt

1 tsp baking soda

¾ cup / 240g plum jam

Confectioners' sugar for sprinkling

Chopped dried fruits and nuts for serving (optional)

In a small saucepan over low heat, combine the milk, both honeys, and butter and bring to a simmer, stirring occasionally, until the butter has melted. Remove from the heat and set aside to cool until lukewarm.

In a large nonmetal bowl, combine the honey mixture, egg, flour, spice blend, 1 pinch salt, and baking soda and stir vigorously until combined and sticky. Cover the bowl with a kitchen towel, and place in the refrigerator for at least 1 week, but preferably for 2 to 3 weeks.

About 1 hour before you're ready to bake, remove the dough from the fridge and set it on the counter at room temperature to take off the chill.

Recipe continues

Preheat the oven to 325°F / 170°C. Line a baking sheet with parchment paper.

Using a spatula, spread the dough on the prepared baking sheet and form it into an 8 by 12-inch / 20 by 30cm rectangle. Bake until the top is just slightly browned and a toothpick inserted into the center comes out with a few moist crumbs, about 20 minutes. During the last few minutes of baking, check the color often so it doesn't become too brown; tent with aluminum foil if necessary. Remove the cake from the oven, place on a wire rack, and let cool to room temperature.

Carefully invert the cake onto a serving platter and, using a sharp knife, trim any uneven edges, then divide the cake into four equal rectangles.

Spread the plum jam on top of three of the rectangles and arrange the rectangles one on top of the other, then top with the plain fourth rectangle. Gently press the top and sides of the cake with the palm of your hand to settle and keep the layers even.

Cover the cake with parchment paper and weigh down the top with a wooden board. Let the cake sit in a cool place for 24 hours to let the flavors develop.

When ready to serve, sprinkle the cake with the confectioners' sugar and top with dried fruits and nuts, if desired, before slicing.

NOTE: If you don't want to make your own spice blend, you can use store-bought gingerbread spice instead.

VARIATION: To make a marzipan version, add a layer of marzipan instead of plum jam to the second cake layer. If you'd like to make your own marzipan, combine 3½ oz / 100g fine almond meal, ¾ cup / 100g confectioners' sugar, and 2 Tbsp water or vodka (or as needed to moisten and form a crumbly dough) and knead until it can be incorporated and formed into a smooth ball. Using a rolling pin, roll out the mixture into a rectangle the exact size of a cake layer and about 1/16 inch / 2mm thick. Arrange the marzipan layer as the second layer when assembling the cake.

Cookies from the Land of a Thousand Fables

The roads into and out of Beauclair are largely safe from banditry due to frequent patrols by knights-errant. Navigating the corridors of the ducal palace, on the other hand, carries a good deal of risk. Two little girls, daughters of the ducal *camerlengo*, claimed the vicinity of the library as their territory and demanded a "toll" from any adventurer who dared enter their domain. The cost of passage? A fairy tale or a sweet treat. For my first toll, I shared the tale of a magic fern flower. Yet my supply of fairy tales quickly ran dry, so I had no other option but to have oat cookies always at the ready. Louis, the palace chef and my friend, frequently supplied me with these crunchy treats, loaded with butter, nuts, and dried fruit. Flattered by my seemingly limitless appetite for these uncomplicated yet scrumptious cookies, he was glad to churn out fresh batches regularly . . . for a time. Eventually, he decided to give me the recipe instead. The girls dubbed them "Cookies from the Land of a Thousand Fables," named for a magical land, the entrance to which they sought in secret, using books they had stolen from the palace library.

MAKES ABOUT 20 COOKIES

1 Tbsp flaxseeds
3 Tbsp lukewarm water
5 Tbsp / 75g unsalted butter, at room temperature, cubed
5 Tbsp / 60g granulated sugar
1⅓ cups / 135g rolled oats
⅓ cup / 40g whole-wheat flour
⅓ cup / 30g chopped nuts (such as walnuts or hazelnuts)
⅓ cup / 50g chopped dried cranberries
1 pinch kosher salt

In a small bowl, combine the flaxseeds and water and set aside until they turn gel-like, about 15 minutes.

In a large bowl, using a wooden spoon, combine the butter and sugar and cream them together until light and fluffy, then mix in the flaxseed mixture. Add the oats, flour, nuts, cranberries, and salt and mix thoroughly, until the dough gets a little sticky. Cover the bowl with a clean kitchen towel and place in the fridge for 30 minutes.

Preheat the oven to 350°F / 180°C. Line a baking sheet with parchment paper.

Remove the dough from the fridge, stir a few times with the wooden spoon, and then roll the dough between your palms to form walnut-sized balls. Arrange the balls on the prepared baking sheet, leaving about 4 inches / 10cm of space between them. Using your palm, flatten each ball into a circle, doubling its diameter and forming a nice cookie shape.

Bake the cookies until the edges are golden brown, about 25 minutes. During the last 5 minutes of baking, check often so the cookies don't get too brown; tent with aluminum foil if necessary. Remove the baking sheet from the oven, place on a wire rack, and let the cookies cool completely.

Store in an airtight container at room temperature for up to 1 week.

TOUSSAINT

Open a crate delivered from afar, forage amidst the straw you find there and draw out a dark-tinted bottle. If you are lucky your wine will taste of Toussaint, a land just south of the Amell Mountains. Each sip will taste of a warm breeze, of the lazily circling wings of a windmill, of the surrounding sunflower meadows. Complex flavors and subtle notes will evoke timeless moments spent in charming villages and castle vineyards that dapple the area's lusciously verdant valleys. Toussaint boasts a plethora of vineyards, but Corvo Bianco, Vermentino, Tufo, Belgaard, Castel Ravello and Pomerol are widely recognized as producers of the Continent's finest wines, exported to its farthest reaches. The land's cuisine, strongly influenced by grape cultivation and bountiful harvests of various crops, is just as remarkable as the prized crimson nectar maturing in sealed barrels. To taste and learn the differences between the *haute cuisine* of Toussaint's capital, Beauclair, and the lands beyond its walls, one need but stroll along the Sansretour River, accompanied by a chorus of cicadas. Unsure of one's path, one can always inquire with the knights-errant who regularly patrol these routes. They invariably prove delightful guides, ever eager to suggest local taverns and inns offering Toussaint's culinary gems—an eclectic array of dishes produced from recipes passed down and perfected from generation to generation.

Double Veggie Ratatouille

Though I was rather pleased with the results of my work over the preceding few weeks, I had not expected my employers to demonstrate their gratitude so emphatically. Yet on the day I completed things, in addition to the agreed-upon fee, the chamberlain presented me with an ample bonus and conveyed the duchess' personal thanks. Her highness, aware of my plans to venture out of the city into the Toussaint countryside, had kindly directed missives to the duchy's finest vineyards and mansions, requesting they treat me as their special guest. A few days on, I arrived at my first stop—the Castel Ravello vineyard. After exchanging pleasantries with the proprietor, I was invited to sample the estate's famous Est Est and Fiorano wines as well as a delicious ratatouille, a signature dish of the region served on tables both noble and peasant. This comforting meal consists of a double portion of vegetables—a base of root veggies topped with a carefully arranged layer of tomatoes and other local produce, all sliced—that is then drizzled with fresh olive oil flavored with herbs and lemon juice.

MAKES 4 SERVINGS

1 medium carrot, diced
1 medium parsley root or parsnip, diced
1 medium celery root, diced
1 small round white potato, diced
2 garlic cloves
2 Tbsp vegetable oil
Kosher salt
1 medium zucchini, thinly sliced
1 medium eggplant, thinly sliced
2 medium tomatoes, thinly sliced

HERB DRIZZLE
3 Tbsp extra-virgin olive oil
1 Tbsp lemon juice
1 tsp dried basil
½ tsp dried thyme
½ tsp dried savory
½ tsp parsley flakes
1 pinch kosher salt

—

Fresh rosemary leaves, for garnish
Fresh bread for serving

Preheat the oven to 400°F / 200°C.

In a 10-inch / 25cm oval ovenproof baking dish, combine the carrot, parsley root, celery root, potato, and garlic, then drizzle with the vegetable oil, sprinkle with ½ tsp salt, and toss to coat. Transfer to the oven and roast the vegetables until soft and lightly browned, about 30 minutes.

Meanwhile, line a baking sheet with parchment paper.

Place the zucchini, eggplant, and tomatoes on the prepared baking sheet and sprinkle both sides of the vegetables with salt. Let sit for 20 minutes, and then pat dry with paper towels. Set aside.

TO MAKE THE DRIZZLE: In a small bowl, combine the olive oil, lemon juice, basil, thyme, savory, parsley flakes, and salt and stir to incorporate. Set aside.

Recipe continues

Remove the root vegetables from the oven and leave the oven on. Peel the garlic and return it to the baking dish. Using a potato masher or a fork, mash the roasted vegetables, season with pepper, and mix to incorporate.

Using a spatula, evenly spread the mashed vegetables across the bottom of the dish. Arrange the zucchini, eggplant, and tomatoes on top of the mashed vegetables in an alternating pattern, starting from the outer edge of the dish and spiraling into the middle. Brush the vegetables with the herb drizzle.

Bake the vegetables, uncovered, until nicely browned, 35 to 40 minutes. Remove from the oven and let rest for 5 minutes.

Garnish with fresh rosemary and serve the ratatouille with hunks of fresh bread.

Fox Hollow Toast with Herbs

Taking advantage of the sunny weather, the next day I set out to explore more of the valley, capturing Toussaint's fairytale landscapes in simple drawings in my journal. For my lunch I had brought along a basket containing a bottle of light wine from the neighboring Vermentino vineyard and crispy, fragrant sourdough toast prepared by the winery's staff. The proprietress had explained how to achieve the unpretentious yet rich flavor—by grinding plenty of local greens, seeds, and oils into a paste, then toasting this with the bread and topping each warm batch with grated, mature cheese. This modest meal, often enjoyed by local workers, originates from the village of Fox Hollow, where it remains a popular choice at the Ruddy Brush Auberge. When I returned the empty basket to its owner, she invited me to sit down to an evening feast. Seated on empty wine crates and sampling appetizers made from local produce, we listened to a wandering storyteller recount some local folktales, including one about a black cat that granted seven wishes and another about a brilliant rat that ran Beauclair's most prestigious tavern, creating culinary wonders from the simplest ingredients.

——————◆———— MAKES 4 SERVINGS ————◆——————

2 garlic cloves, minced

½ tsp kosher salt

2 Tbsp sunflower seeds, finely chopped

1½ cups / 70g chopped fresh flat-leaf parsley

¾ cup / 40g chopped arugula

6 Tbsp / 15g finely chopped basil

2 Tbsp extra-virgin olive oil, with more for drizzling

1 Tbsp unsalted butter, melted

1 loaf sourdough bread

Grated hard cheese (such as Grana Padano
  or Parmesan) for sprinkling

———————◇———————

In a mortar with a pestle, grind together the garlic and salt and then add the sunflower seeds and grind again. Once everything is finely ground, add the parsley, arugula, basil, olive oil, and butter and grind again, until the mixture is the consistency of paste. Set aside.

Preheat the oven to 300°F / 150°C. Line a baking sheet with parchment paper.

Cut the bread into twelve slices and arrange on the prepared baking sheet. Drizzle with a little olive oil.

Bake the bread for 5 minutes. Remove the pan from the oven, generously spread the herb mix on top of each slice, and return the pan to the oven. Continue to bake until slightly browned on top, 8 to 10 minutes more.

Sprinkle the toasts with grated cheese and serve immediately.

NOTE: Although not a traditional addition, for those who prefer more zing, stir a little lemon zest into the herb mixture.

Dun Tynne Leek and Bacon Soup

I arrived at Dun Tynne Castle a few hours after sunset, having previously taken a wrong turn at a crossroads. While my room was being prepared, I was led to the kitchen where the cook heated a bowl of leek soup for me. The creamy vegetable broth proved to be delicious. Chunks of smoked bacon garnished with caramelized leek strips, droplets of fine olive oil, and nigella seeds produced a warm, delectable harmony. Nourished but fatigued, I sought out my assigned quarters, though with only a candle to light my way, the task was not easy. After many minutes of searching, I opened what I believed to be the door to my room only to find myself face-to-face with the silhouette of a woman hovering in the twilight. I dropped my candle in terror and stepped back into a suit of armor, which crashed to the floor and awoke all the members of the household within earshot. Once the staff had brought more light, I asked, mortified, whom I should apologize to for breaking into their room. I was told that the quarters were now vacant, but had once belonged to the owner's ancestor Téofila, whose portrait hung in the castle's main dining hall. The ghost, whom locals call the "Lady in White," is said to emerge from her painted representation just before midnight to stalk the corridors and visit the castle's nooks and crannies.

MAKES 4 SERVINGS

2 large leeks (white and green parts), trimmed and halved

5 oz / 150g slab bacon, diced

2 celery stalks, diced

2 garlic cloves, minced

3 cups / 720ml vegetable stock or water, or as needed

2 medium round white potatoes, diced

1 bay leaf

1 sprig rosemary, or ½ tsp dried rosemary

Kosher salt

3 Tbsp sour cream

1 tsp parsley flakes

Freshly ground black pepper

Extra-virgin olive oil for drizzling

Chopped chives for garnishing

1 tsp nigella seeds (optional)

Rinse the leeks thoroughly, then drain and thinly slice crosswise.

In a medium stockpot over medium heat, combine the bacon and a splash of cold water. Cook, stirring occasionally, until the water evaporates, 2 to 3 minutes, then continue cooking until the fat renders and the bacon is lightly browned, 4 to 5 minutes more. Add the leeks and celery and cook, stirring occasionally, until the vegetables soften and are lightly browned, another 4 to 5 minutes. Then add the garlic and stir-fry for 30 seconds.

Turn the heat to high and add the vegetable stock, potatoes, bay leaf, rosemary, and 1 tsp salt and bring to a boil. Turn the heat to low, cover, and let simmer until the potatoes are completely tender, about 15 minutes. Discard the bay leaf and rosemary sprig (if using).

Recipe continues

Using a potato masher, lightly mash the soup until it becomes thick but has some chunks remaining.

In a small bowl, combine ¼ cup / 60ml of the hot soup and the sour cream, stir to incorporate, and then slowly pour this mixture into the pot, while stirring constantly with a wooden spoon (to prevent curdling of the cream). Stir in the parsley flakes and continue to simmer for

3 minutes more. If the soup is too thick, add additional vegetable stock. Season with additional salt, if needed, and pepper.

Ladle the soup into individual bowls, drizzle with olive oil, and garnish with chives and the nigella seeds, if desired. Serve immediately.

Gélenser Radish and Cabbage Slaw

Following the unfortunate incident at Dun Tynne Castle the evening before, by way of apology I offered to help in the kitchen the next day. At first my hosts would not hear of a guest taking up any sort of labor, but they gave in once I assured them of my passion for the culinary arts and eagerness to learn local recipes. One of the kitchen hands had the day off. As the cook told it, the girl was squandering her leisure time weaving a nettle shirt that would, she hoped, lift a curse from a swan that called *Mare Aubrebis* Lake home. In any case, I was asked to assist in the preparation of a local radish and cabbage slaw. Under the cook's guidance, I went through the recipe's vital steps—macerating finely shredded cabbage in salt and marinating slices of radish and thin strips of carrot in honey and vinegar. As I completed the dish, a knight-errant appeared unexpectedly. He had been patrolling the area around the castle and had unfortunate news for both myself and the cook. A slyzard recently spotted in the Caroberta Woods had been forcing travelers to take long detours. Now it also jeopardized the future radish-based menu by cutting off deliveries from the Gélenser Farmstead, famed for cultivating the best radishes in all Toussaint.

MAKES 4 SERVINGS

HONEY–VINEGAR MARINADE
2 tsp floral honey
¼ cup / 60ml apple cider vinegar or
  lemon juice, or as needed
2 pinches kosher salt
—
10 radishes, trimmed and thinly sliced
1 medium carrot, cut into long, thin strips
7 oz / 200g red cabbage, cored and shredded
7 oz / 200g green cabbage, cored and shredded
Kosher salt
½ leek (white and green parts), trimmed and halved
¼ cup / 15g chopped fresh dill
2 sprigs chopped flat-leaf parsley

3 Tbsp extra-virgin olive oil
Freshly ground black pepper
2 Tbsp sunflower seeds
A splash of apple cider vinegar (optional)

TO MAKE THE MARINADE: In a small bowl, combine the honey, vinegar, and salt and whisk to incorporate.

Add the radishes and carrot to the marinade, toss to coat, and then set aside for 30 minutes.

Recipe continues

In a large bowl, combine both cabbages and 1 tsp salt, toss a few times to incorporate, cover, and set aside until the cabbages have softened a bit, about 20 minutes.

Meanwhile, rinse the leek thoroughly, then drain and thinly slice crosswise.

Strain the radishes and carrot and reserve the marinade. Place the radishes and carrot in the bowl with the cabbages and add the leek, dill, and parsley.

Add the olive oil and ½ tsp pepper to the marinade and whisk thoroughly to combine, then pour over the vegetables and toss to coat. Set this slaw aside for 5 minutes.

Warm a small nonstick dry skillet over medium heat. Add the sunflower seeds and toast, shaking the pan occasionally, until slightly browned, about 1 minute. Set aside to cool.

Add the sunflower seeds to the slaw bowl and toss to combine. Taste and season with salt, pepper, and the vinegar, if needed.

Serve the slaw immediately.

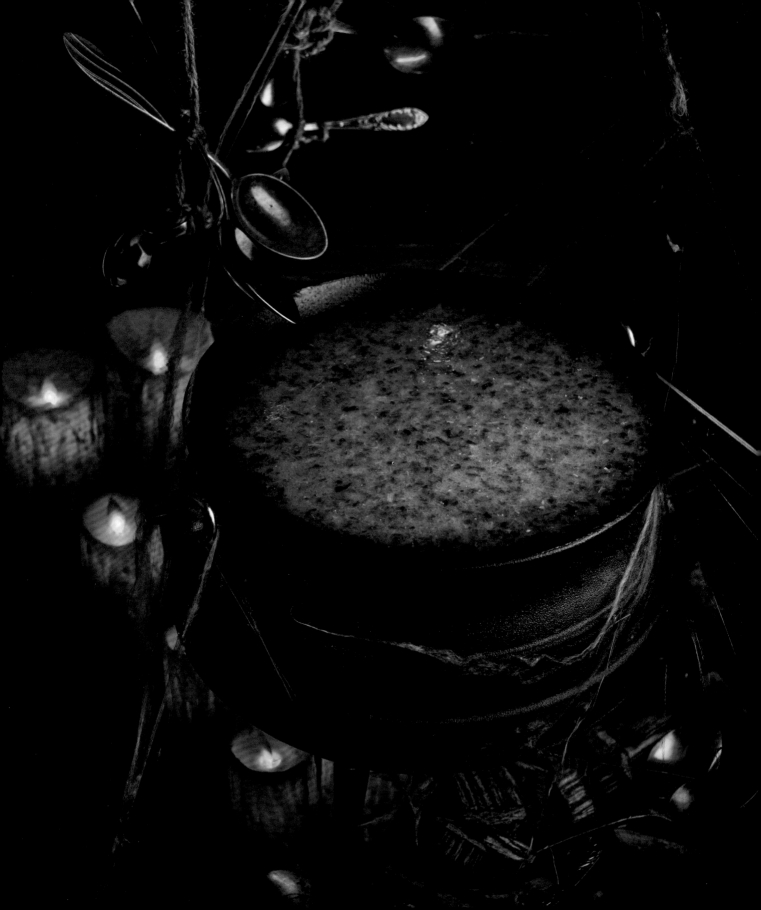

Wight's Sorrel Soup

The story of this recipe is so astonishing that few of my relatives at home in Kovir will believe it. At dusk, rather than returning to the castle via the shorter path along the Dun Tynne hillside, I took another trail leading past the cemetery on the slope of Mont Crane. There, I encountered a girl lugging a heavy cauldron. After a brief conversation, I offered to help carry it. As it turned out, she was the aforementioned kitchen hand from the castle, though the cook had been sorely mistaken about the reason for her absence. Though she in truth had been collecting wild plants from roadside ditches, it was sorrel, not nettles, she was gathering for a nourishing recipe. The green-hued soup she aimed to make based on a pork-rib broth was for her brother. He had been cursed, and no one had thus far found a remedy. The poor wretch was forced to seek seclusion in a cemetery and await meals brought by his family, who would announce their arrival with the clanging of spoons hung on a string. Though the pungent, green broth initially repulsed me, the story nevertheless inspired me to include this sorrel soup recipe in my journal. The refined result proved surprisingly delicious with the addition of cream and hard-boiled eggs. It should be noted that, despite similar origins, this unusual soup is much tastier than the one from *The Adventures of Spikey and a Wight called Franconi*.

—◁ MAKES 4 SERVINGS ▷—

RIB STOCK
1 lb / 450g pork ribs
2 qt / 2L water
2 medium carrots, halved
2 parsley roots or parsnips, halved
1 celery stalk, halved
1 medium yellow onion, halved
1 leek (white and green parts), trimmed
   and halved lengthwise
1 bay leaf
2 allspice berries
1½ tsp kosher salt

—

1 Tbsp unsalted butter
One 10.6-oz / 300g jar brined sorrel (see Note)
7 Tbsp / 100ml heavy cream
Kosher salt and freshly ground black pepper
Hard-boiled eggs or mashed potatoes for serving

TO MAKE THE STOCK: Wash the pork ribs under cold running water, place in a large saucepan over high heat, cover with the 2 qt / 2L water, and bring to a boil. Turn the heat to low and bring to a simmer. Using a slotted spoon, occasionally skim and discard any accumulated foam from the surface. After 30 minutes, add the carrots, parsley roots, celery, onion, leek, bay leaf, allspice berries, and salt. Cover and continue to simmer until the meat and vegetables are soft, about 1½ hours. Strain the stock. Discard the meat and vegetables (see Note), then return the remaining stock to the saucepan.

In a medium nonstick skillet over medium heat, melt the butter. Add the sorrel with its brine and stir-fry for 3 minutes, then stir into the strained stock and let simmer, uncovered, for 10 minutes.

Recipe continues

Gradually pour the cream into the saucepan while stirring vigorously with a wooden spoon. Season with salt and pepper, if desired, and continue to simmer for 3 to 5 minutes.

Ladle the soup into individual bowls. Serve immediately with hard-boiled egg halves or mashed potatoes on the side.

NOTES

You can use up the meat from the stock by pulling it from the cooked rib bones and adding to the soup or eating it separately with hunks of bread. And you can make a simple salad with the cooked vegetables, except for the leek and onion, by dicing them and then combining with mayonnaise, diced Brined Cucumbers (page 83), and chopped apples. Season with salt and pepper.

If you can't find brined sorrel, use ½ lb / 225g of chopped fresh sorrel.

Flamiche

The village of Flovive was named after a raftsman named Flavien. According to legend, he saved the duchy from a plague of frogs by serenading the amphibians on his fiddle and coaxing them to follow him beyond its confines. Each year, a multi-day festival is held to commemorate this event, which I very much wished to attend. Upon my arrival in Flovive, I decided, as usual, to sample the local cuisine while watching a musicians' parade inaugurate the festivities. At the Barrel and Bung, they served *flamiche*, a dish that has been the villagers' pride for years and, like everything in Toussaint, has a story behind its inception. It apparently all began with an unfortunate mishap. As a Tufo vineyard worker's wife was entering the village square, she tripped and fell, causing the eggs, cheese, and cream in her basket to blend together. A friend came to her aid and suggested they rescue the mess by removing any eggshells and baking the mish-mashed ingredients with the bread dough the friend had been kneading. The current version of *flamiche* enriches the traditional base of fluffy dough with its creamy filling by adding leeks stewed in local white wine. The dish is enjoyed both as a snack and as a main meal in many households throughout the duchy.

◄——— MAKES 6 SERVINGS ———►

YEAST STARTER
3 Tbsp whole milk
½ tsp granulated sugar
1 tsp instant yeast, or 8g fresh yeast, crumbled
2 Tbsp all-purpose flour

—

1½ cups / 210g all-purpose flour, with more for sprinkling
⅔ cup / 160ml whole milk, lukewarm
¾ tsp kosher salt
2 Tbsp extra-virgin olive oil

FILLING
1 large leek (white and light-green parts), trimmed and halved lengthwise
1 Tbsp unsalted butter
¼ cup / 60ml dry or semidry white wine
3 pinches kosher salt
4½ Tbsp / 70ml crème fraîche (see Note) or sour cream
2 eggs
2½ oz / 70g hard cheese (such as Gruyère), finely grated
1 generous pinch freshly grated nutmeg
1 pinch freshly ground black pepper

TO MAKE THE STARTER: In a medium bowl, combine the milk, sugar, and yeast and stir until the yeast is fully dissolved. Add the flour and, using a fork, mix until well combined. Cover the bowl with a kitchen towel and let the starter sit until doubled in size, about 20 minutes.

Lightly flour a work surface.

Add the flour, milk, and salt to the bowl with the yeast starter and stir to incorporate into a crumbly, wet dough. Turn the dough onto the prepared work surface and knead until soft and elastic, 4 to 5 minutes. If the dough is still too sticky, sprinkle with additional flour. At the end of kneading, add the olive oil and a sprinkle of flour and knead until the oil is fully incorporated into the dough.

Form the dough into a ball, cover with the kitchen towel, and let rise until doubled in size, 1½ to 2 hours.

Recipe continues

TO MAKE THE FILLING: While the dough is rising, rinse the leek thoroughly, then drain and cut into ¼-inch / 6mm slices.

In a medium nonstick skillet over medium heat, melt the butter. Add the leek and cook, stirring occasionally until lightly browned, about 4 minutes. Turn the heat to low, pour in the wine, and let simmer until the liquid evaporates, about 3 minutes. Season with 2 pinches of the salt and set aside.

In a small bowl, combine the crème fraîche, eggs, and one-third of the cheese and whisk to incorporate. Season with the nutmeg, pepper, and remaining 1 pinch salt. Add the cooled leek and stir until well combined.

Preheat the oven to 400°F / 200°C.

Once the dough has doubled in size, punch it down and pat it into a round 11-inch / 28cm baking pan or pizza pan. It should be about ⅛-inch / 3mm thick with a ⅓-inch / 1cm raised border all around (like a pizza). Make sure there are no holes in the dough, so the filling can't leak out. Evenly sprinkle the remaining two-thirds cheese over the dough within the border.

Bake the dough for 5 minutes, then pull out the rack and quickly spoon the filling into the center, spreading it up to the border. Return the pan to the oven and continue baking until the filling is fully set and lightly browned, 20 to 25 minutes. During the last minutes of baking, check the color often so the crust doesn't get too brown. Transfer the pan to a wire rack and let rest for 2 minutes to cool slightly. Run a knife around the edges of the pan and then remove the flamiche and cut into six wedges.

Serve the flamiche hot or at room temperature.

NOTE: If you don't have crème fraîche on hand, you can easily make a homemade version. First, sterilize a 1-pint / 500ml jar and its lid with boiling water and then wipe it dry with a paper towel. Pour ¾ cup / 175ml heavy cream and 2 Tbsp buttermilk into the jar and mix thoroughly. Close the jar tightly and let it sit at room temperature for 20 hours for the mixture to thicken. Then put the jar in the refrigerator for 24 hours before using; the mixture will thicken even more and develop a little sour taste.

Store in the refrigerator for up to 7 days.

Francollarts Baguette Platter

Trouble, following age-old custom, appeared when least expected. At the village of Francollarts I was greeted by a throng of merchants and travelers whose route to the Belgaard vineyard had been blocked by a cohort of knights-errant. At a baker's stall, the talkative owner explained the cause of the commotion whilst selling sandwiches to all those waiting. The troublemaker was apparently a squire named Pierre Gynt, who had journeyed to Mount Gorgon and the legendary Hall of the Mountain King to retrieve a jewel for his cherished mademoiselle. Pierre had returned from the cave not with a jewel, but with a curse that blighted the village with mysterious disappearances. Whatever had followed the young squire back, it no doubt complicated my plan to return to the capital. But, as my beloved nana always said, "Just as a cat cannot lay eggs, a man cannot move a mountain." I decided not to fight the circumstances and to wait for the situation to resolve itself. I passed the time by chatting with the baker and sampling his open-faced baguettes. He proudly emphasized that the various toppings were his original ideas, such as creamy camembert, caramelized onions, and nuts, all on toast, or the soft bread with fresh tuna, egg, and herb paste. His opinion of the knights-errant and their handling of the present situation was far less enthusiastic. "Those pompous twits? Only good for jousts and tourneys, I say. When there's serious trouble, we send for a witcher."

TOUSSAINT

─── ► MAKES 6 SERVINGS ◄ ───

FISH PÂTÉ
One 5-oz / 142g can water-packed
   solid white tuna, drained
2 Tbsp mayonnaise
2 hard-boiled eggs, finely chopped
⅓ cup / 20g chopped fresh dill
1 heaping Tbsp chopped fresh flat-leaf parsley
2 chives or green onions, chopped
Kosher salt and freshly ground black pepper

CARAMELIZED ONIONS
2 Tbsp vegetable oil
2 medium red onions, thinly sliced
2 pinches kosher salt
1 Tbsp floral honey
3 Tbsp water, or as needed
1 Tbsp balsamic vinegar
1 pinch dried thyme

6 oz / 170g Camembert cheese
2 fresh baguettes, sliced diagonally ½ inch / 1.3cm thick
Extra-virgin olive oil for brushing
Kosher salt and freshly ground black pepper
¼ cup / 30g chopped walnuts

─── ◇ ───

TO MAKE THE FISH PÂTÉ: In a small bowl, combine the tuna, mayonnaise, eggs, and two-thirds each of the dill, parsley, and chives and, using a fork, thoroughly mash to obtain a paste consistency. Season with salt and pepper. Cover and refrigerate for 30 minutes.

Recipe continues

TO MAKE THE CARAMELIZED ONIONS: In a medium non-stick skillet over medium heat, warm the vegetable oil. Add the onions and salt and cook, stirring occasionally with a wooden spoon, until starting to soften, about 5 minutes. Stir in the honey and water, turn the heat to medium-low, and continue to cook, stirring frequently and scraping the bottom of the pan, until the water has evaporated and the onions are very soft and heavily browned, about 25 minutes. (Add small splashes of water every time the onions start to stick to the pan.) Turn the heat to low, stir in the vinegar and thyme, and continue to cook until all the liquid has evaporated and the onions are sticky, about 5 minutes more. Turn off the heat and set aside.

Preheat the oven to 300°F / 150°C. Line a baking sheet with parchment paper.

Thinly slice the Camembert.

Brush half of the baguette slices with olive oil, add a few slices of Camembert, and sprinkle with salt and pepper. Arrange the slices on the prepared baking sheet.

Bake the topped baguette slices until the Camembert has melted slightly, 5 to 7 minutes, or a little longer if you prefer the cheese to be a little softer. Remove from the oven, transfer the baguettes to a platter. Then add a generous portion of the caramelized onions on top of each slice and garnish with the walnuts.

Remove the pâté from the fridge and arrange generous portions on top of the remaining baguette slices. Garnish the pâté with the remaining dill, parsley, and chives.

Serve the baguettes immediately.

The Cockatrice Inn's Hare Pâté

"Every journey begins with a first step. Take it at the Cockatrice Inn." This advertisement alone—pinned to a notice board alongside a note about a found dog named Spot—convinced me to visit the establishment situated on a bridge spanning the Sansretour River. I had been counting on sampling their widely recommended Fisherman's Chowder, but due to a shortage of fresh crayfish I was forced to choose another dish. That is how a portion of fresh hare pâté (supposedly baked for the time it takes to recite two litanies to Saint Plegmund) landed on my table. The savory delicacy with its velvety texture and distinct flavor seemed to melt on my tongue. It also paired surprisingly well with the fruity, red wine-based dessert served alongside it. As I was finishing my meal, I listened to a fierce debate about whether or not the gaze of a cockatrice—whose likeness hung above the inn's doorway—was dangerous. One man, convinced it was lethal, claimed a silver mirror to reflect the gaze was the sole way to protect oneself. Another responded that it was no more dangerous than an angered turkey and instructed his debater to "smash the mirror over his foolish head." Unfortunately (or perhaps fortunately), I did not stay to hear the end of the debate as I set off for the next stop along my route—the Corvo Bianco vineyard.

———————◀ MAKES 10 SERVINGS ▶———————

1½ lb / 700g hare or rabbit legs
12 oz / 350g chicken leg
3½ oz / 100g slab bacon, cubed
Lukewarm water as needed
2 bay leaves
2 allspice berries
5 black peppercorns
1 medium yellow onion, halved
1 medium carrot, halved
1 parsley root or parsnip, halved
Kosher salt
½ oz / 15g dried mushroom slices
   (such as bay bolete or porcini)
2 slices stale white bread, or 1 stale roll
7 oz / 200g chicken livers
1 Tbsp vegetable oil or lard, with more
   for greasing (optional)
Freshly ground black pepper
¼ cup / 15g chopped fresh flat-leaf parsley

1 Tbsp dried marjoram, or as needed
1 tsp ground ginger, or as needed
2 pinches freshly grated nutmeg, or as needed
3 eggs, separated
2 to 3 Tbsp chicken stock or vegetable stock (optional)
Bread crumbs for sprinkling
Sliced fresh bread for serving

———————◇———————

In a large Dutch oven over high heat, combine the hare legs, chicken leg, and bacon and cook until slightly browned, about 2 minutes, then flip the meat and cook for 2 minutes more. Turn the heat to low, pour in enough water to cover the meat, then add the bay leaves, allspice berries, and peppercorns. Cover and let simmer for about 1 hour. Add the onion, carrot, and parsley root and continue to simmer until the meat becomes soft and

Recipe continues

starts to fall off the bones, about 1 hour more. About 15 minutes before the end of cooking, add 2 tsp salt and stir gently.

Meanwhile, rinse the mushrooms with cold water, place in a small bowl, cover with lukewarm water, and let soak for 40 minutes. Strain and reserve the soaking water. Set mushrooms aside.

Strain the meat and vegetables, reserving the stock, and let cool. When the hare legs and chicken leg are lukewarm, pull the meat from the bones. Discard the bones, skin, bay leaves, allspice berries, and peppercorns. Transfer the meat to a big bowl, along with the cooked vegetables and bacon, and set aside.

In a separate small bowl, combine the bread with some of the reserved stock and let soak for 20 minutes. Then drain the bread, squeeze out the excess liquid, and add to the bowl with the meat and vegetables.

Trim and discard any connective tissue and fat residue from the livers, halve the larger livers so all the pieces are of similar size, and then pat dry with paper towels.

In a medium nonstick skillet over medium-high heat, warm the vegetable oil. Add the livers and cook until browned, about 2 minutes. Then, using tongs, flip the livers (being careful not to puncture them) and cook for 2 minutes more. Turn the heat to low, add the drained mushrooms and 1 to 2 Tbsp of their soaking water, stir, and continue to cook until the water has evaporated, about 2 minutes more. Turn off the heat, season with a pinch each of salt and pepper, transfer the livers and mushrooms to the bowl with the meat and vegetables, and let cool to room temperature.

When the ingredients have cooled, pass the meat-vegetable mixture through a meat grinder three times or, using a food processor, pulse the mixture until it

has a smooth, uniform consistency, like a thick purée. Transfer the meat mixture to a bowl; add the parsley, marjoram, ginger, nutmeg, 1 tsp salt, and 1 tsp pepper; and, using a fork, mix thoroughly. Taste and season with additional salt and spices, if desired; it should be well seasoned at this point. Add the egg yolks and stir to incorporate.

Preheat the oven to 350°F / 180°C. Line a 9 by 5-inch / 23 by 13cm loaf pan or terrine with parchment paper or grease with vegetable oil. Sprinkle with bread crumbs.

Place the egg whites in a medium metal bowl, add a pinch of salt, and, using a whisk, whip into stiff peaks.

Using a spatula, gently fold the egg whites into the meat mixture. Check the consistency; it should be well combined and moist but not runny—a good indicator is if you hear squelching sounds when you tap the top with your fingers. If it's too dry, stir in the chicken stock as needed; if it's too moist, sprinkle in some bread crumbs. Transfer the mixture to the prepared pan, and then, using your palm, flatten the top.

Bake the pâté for 15 minutes. Then turn the oven temperature to 300°F / 150°C and continue baking until golden brown on top, 60 to 70 minutes. If the top begins to get too brown, cover it with a piece of parchment paper or aluminum foil. At the end of baking, poke a wooden skewer into the middle of the pâté—if the skewer comes out clean, the pâté is ready; if not, continue cooking for a few minutes more.

Let the pâté cool to room temperature, then run a knife around the edges and invert onto a cutting board or serving plate. It can be served right away, but if refrigerated overnight, it will become firmer and will have a richer flavor. Serve with slices of freshly baked bread.

Wine Kissel

Kissel is a gooey, ruby-colored ostensible dessert with bits of cranberry, raspberry, and cherry. I was able to sample it at the Cockatrice Inn, where it tickled my taste buds so thoroughly that it came to deserve its own entry in my journal. It proved intriguing not just due to its sweet-yet-sour flavor, derived from the combination of ripe fruit with a base of red wine, but also through its unconventional use in the local cuisine. While you will find cranberry kissel served solely as a dessert on Redanian tables, in Toussaint chefs tend to approach cooking more as an art than a craft. So they use kissel as a sauce to accompany various savory dishes. Not least among them, the hare pâté I was served at the Cockatrice.

⤞ MAKES 2 SERVINGS ⤜

½ cup / 120ml dry or semidry red wine
⅔ cup / 80g fresh or frozen raspberries
⅓ cup / 25g fresh or frozen sour cherries, pitted
1½ Tbsp dried cranberries
½ cup / 120ml water
2 Tbsp potato starch
1 Tbsp floral honey
1 pinch kosher salt
1 pinch ground cloves (optional)
Whipped cream for serving (optional)

In a medium saucepan over low heat, combine the wine, raspberries, cherries, cranberries, and ¼ cup / 60ml of the water and slowly bring to a simmer.

In a liquid measuring cup, combine the remaining ¼ cup / 60ml water and the potato starch, whisk to incorporate, and then slowly pour it into the saucepan, while stirring constantly. Bring the mixture to a simmer, stirring frequently, and cook until it thickens and resembles fruit jelly, about 2 minutes. Turn off the heat; add the honey, salt, and cloves (if using); and stir to combine. Pour the mixture into small bowls or cups and let cool.

Serve the kissel slightly chilled or at room temperature, topped with a dollop of whipped cream, if desired.

VARIATION: To use this as an accompaniment for meats, such as Hare Pâté (page 217), decrease the potato starch by half and replace the ¼ cup / 60ml water with an additional 2 Tbsp red wine. Continue as directed but omit the honey. Once the mixture has boiled, mash the fruits with a fork for a thicker consistency. Set aside to cool before serving.

Corvo Bianco Lemonade

The walk from the Cockatrice Inn to the Corvo Bianco vineyard was pleasant, even in the sweltering heat of the day. I was eager to sample the vineyard's wine, true, but above all to exchange a few words with its extraordinary owner. For Corvo Bianco belongs to Geralt of Rivia himself, the famous White Wolf, a witcher whose exploits are known throughout the Northern Realms, from Kovir in the far north to the Amell Mountains (and, as it turned out, beyond them) in the south. Apart from meeting the legendary monster-slayer in person, I hoped to ask him about a peculiar journal I had acquired in Oxenfurt. Sadly, I would be disappointed. When at last I arrived at the vineyard, its exceedingly polite majordomo informed me that its owner was not expected to return for weeks at the least, if not until the end of autumn, just before the first heavy snows would block the mountain passes. Crestfallen, I nonetheless accepted the majordomo's invitation to rest my weary legs. I spent a few hours in the shade of a rose-covered arbor, sipping lemonade squeezed from ripe lemons, then blended with the juice of freshly picked white grapes. This delicious mixture, common in the region, is customarily served as a refreshment during the grape harvest. Meanwhile, I listened to a story about the origins of the vineyard and the famed Sepremento wine it had once produced, and of how Geralt of Rivia came to be the property's owner, transforming the run-down estate into a once more respected and prospering one. Only once the fiery sunset had given way to the evening's cool palette did I bid farewell to Corvo Bianco's hospitality and turn my gaze and steps toward Beauclair's city gates. I did not doubt the majordomo regarding Geralt of Rivia's prolonged absence. Yet as I strode down the road I secretly hoped one of the travelers I passed would turn out to be a white-haired man with two swords on his back.

MAKES 1 QUART / 1L

2½ cups / 600ml 100 percent white grape juice
Juice of 2 lemons, plus 1 lemon, sliced
1 cup / 150g white grapes, stemmed and halved
Floral honey for sweetening (optional)
10 mint leaves, with more for garnishing

In a 1-qt / 1L pitcher with a lid, combine the grape juice and lemon juice, then add the lemon slices, grape halves, and mint. Cover and refrigerate for at least 1 hour or up to 2 days before serving.

When ready to serve, sweeten with honey, if needed, and garnish with the mint leaves.

The Cooking Secrets of Witchers
For Dealing with Hardships and Struggles Beyond Monster-Slaying

Oxenfurt, after Midaëte, *the end of June*
Dense clouds loom in the sky, so the season of storms has clearly begun. Thus the whims of fickle nature have greatly extended my stay in Oxenfurt. Trapped in the city and unable to embark on the next stage of my journey, I have accepted an offer from the antique shop of an auction house to restore an old map of unknown provenance. I was working in the shop the other day when an old, weathered, leather-bound journal caught my eye. The antique dealer acquired it shortly after the Battle of Brenna, and it allegedly belonged to a fallen witcher named Coën, as evidenced by the former owner's initials inscribed inside the front cover. The surviving entries are so illegible and incomplete as to be very difficult to decipher. So it has been gathering dust in the antique shop for years, classified rather as a curio than a valuable artifact that could become the object of a vigorous bidding contest. Still, it intrigues me enough that I have requested it be made part of the payment for my work, hoping that I might one day decipher its contents.

Novigrad, July, three weeks after summer solstice
For the first time since acquiring the journal, I found the time to study it more closely recently. Interestingly, the surviving pages have turned out to contain fragments of recipes, listing herbs, spices, and ingredients, though it will take me some time to excavate the owner's faded scrawls.

Beauclair, after the Lammas *harvest holiday, August*
Due to rough seas, I found it impossible to work on deciphering the journal's contents during my journey to and from the Skellige Isles. I have been forced to wait to resume my efforts until now, when I have reached dry land. Still, I find myself in a bit of a pickle, for the journal's tantalizing inscriptions are proving difficult to unravel. Might another witcher fare better in making sense of its contents? They say a rather famed one resides in the vicinity of Beauclair.

Toussaint, before the Velen *holiday, September*
Unfortunately, my hopes of finding a witcher to help me decipher Coën's journal have been dashed. Corvo Bianco's owner is absent, it is unclear when he will return. But as I do not give up easily, I shall continue working on this peculiar puzzle as I make my way back to Kovir. Eventually, I will lift its fragments out of cursed obscurity, shining the beam of careful scrutiny and understanding upon them.

En route to Kovir, three days to the Saovine *holiday*
I have managed to reconstruct and organize most of the decipherable journal entries. The surviving fragments contain not, as I thought earlier, secret witcher notes, but simple recipes—perhaps once prepared in the kitchens of Kaer Morhen itself. I have decided that I will include them in my own journal, as they, too, represent a kind of culinary journey. This one to a distant corner of the Continent I myself did not reach. Coën's notes pry open, if only slightly, the mighty door to the legendary witchers' stronghold . . .

KAER MORHEN

If one unfurls a map under the faint gleam of candlelight, tracing with one's finger the lines and swirls of ink that are the Continent's contours, betwixt its cities, villages, mountains and forests there remain many uncharted, empty spaces to discover. For reasons known to a select few, these regions were never thoroughly mapped or intentionally left to the imagination as sources of speculation and myth. Similarly, a fog of mystery surrounds witchers, their guild and their legendary stronghold of Kaer Morhen. If tales recounted among villagers or gossip circulating in royal courts hold any truth, this isolated fortress lies hidden among the wild peaks of the Blue Mountains, along the course of the Gwenllech River, in the farthest reaches of Kaedwen's borderlands. For several centuries the stronghold, at present said to be in ruins, was the seat of the famous School of the Wolf. As rumors contend, its paltry few remaining masters still reconvene within Kaer Morhen's walls for harsh winters.

Geralt's Omelet for Yennefer

The best, fluffiest wyvern egg omelets are served at the Country Inn near Vizima. I had the privilege of tasting them myself thanks to my relatives' recommendation. In my version, using more readily available chicken eggs, I whisk only half the eggs to maintain a perfect balance between fluffiness and creaminess. When greater hunger strikes, I would suggest adding ham or fried bacon, a diced handful of either or both.

Nutritious breakfast from Aedd Gynvael. Golden Sturgeon, maybe? Not sure where Geralt found the recipe. I've only ever known him to have scrambled eggs in taverns. Apparently Yennefer's cravings made him try something different . . . Still can't trust him as a cook, though. He's lousy. Goes to soft-boil eggs, half the time he forgets to add water. But this recipe gives you a fluffy omelet. Delicious, really. Geralt's instructions are basic, though. He didn't exactly exploit our pantry's potential. Add ingredients to make it really good.

MAKES 1 SERVING

1 Tbsp vegetable oil
⅓ medium yellow onion, thinly sliced
⅓ red bell pepper, cored and thinly sliced
Kosher salt and freshly ground black pepper
2 tsp unsalted butter
3 cremini mushrooms, sliced
2 eggs; 1 separated
⅓ cup / 30g shredded cheese (such as Cheddar or Gruyère)
Leaves from several sprigs flat-leaf parsley, chopped
Fresh bread for serving

*eggs
onions
mushrooms
cheese
herbs
butter*

In a small nonstick skillet over medium heat, warm the vegetable oil. Add the onion and bell pepper and cook, stirring occasionally, until soft and browned, about 5 minutes. Season with salt and black pepper, transfer to a small bowl, cover, and set aside.

In the same skillet over medium heat, melt 1 tsp of the butter. Add the mushrooms to the skillet and cook for 2 minutes until lightly browned, then flip and continue to cook until browned on the other side. Season with salt and black pepper and transfer to the bowl with the onion and bell pepper. Cover the bowl and set aside.

Crack one of the eggs into a small bowl. Add the remaining egg yolk and whisk together. In a separate small metal bowl, combine the remaining egg white and a pinch of salt and, using a whisk, whip into soft peaks. Add one-third of the whipped white to the bowl with the whisked egg, gently stirring with a spatula to incorporate. Add half the cheese, the parsley, some black pepper, and another pinch of salt and then mix and gently fold in the remaining two-thirds whipped egg white.

In the same skillet over medium heat, melt the remaining 1 tsp butter. Pour in the egg mixture and, using the spatula, spread the mixture evenly across the bottom of the pan. Cover and cook the omelet until the bottom is browned but the top is a little moist, about 5 minutes.

When the omelet is set, sprinkle the remaining cheese over the top, place the fried onion, bell pepper, and mushrooms on one half of the omelet, then carefully fold over the other half to cover. Turn the heat to low, cover the skillet, and cook for 1 minute more. Transfer to a serving plate.

Serve the omelet immediately with hunks of fresh bread.

Vesemir's Bean and Tomato Stew

This creamy stew is the perfect comfort meal for frostier days. If you happen to have spices from the Zerrikanian Spice Company at hand, add a few pinches of red pepper flakes or ground spicy paprika. Do so at the end of cooking to bring more heat to the dish.

———◄ MAKES 4 TO 6 SERVINGS ►———

1½ cups / 280g dried white beans, or two 15.5-oz / 435g cans white beans (drained)

10 cups / 2.4L boiled water, cooled to lukewarm (if using dried beans)

1 bay leaf

2 allspice berries

Kosher salt

1 Tbsp vegetable oil

9 oz / 250g smoked kielbasa, sliced or diced

1 medium yellow onion, diced

3 garlic cloves, minced

1 Tbsp tomato paste

1 cup / 240ml tomato purée

2 tsp dried marjoram, or as needed

1 tsp dried oregano

1 Tbsp unsalted butter

1 Tbsp all-purpose flour

3 Tbsp whipping cream

1 Tbsp floral honey

Freshly ground black pepper

Fresh bread for serving

——————◇——————

If using dried beans, in a large saucepan, combine the beans with 5 cups / 1.2L of the cooled boiled water. Let the beans soak at room temperature for about 10 hours until they double in volume. Drain the soaking liquid, add the remaining 5 cups / 1.2L fresh water, the bay leaf, and allspice berries, and set over high heat. Bring to a boil, then turn the heat to medium and cook, uncovered,

for 10 minutes. Partially cover and turn the heat to medium-low and continue cooking until tender, about 1 hour. Stir in 1 tsp salt about 5 minutes before the end of cooking. Strain, reserving 1 cup / 240ml of the cooking liquid. Discard the bay leaf and allspice berries.

In a medium nonstick skillet over medium heat, warm the vegetable oil. Add the kielbasa and cook, stirring occasionally, until lightly browned, a few minutes. Transfer the kielbasa to a bowl and set aside.

In the same skillet over medium heat, add the onion to the remaining kielbasa fat and cook, stirring occasionally, until lightly browned, about 5 minutes. Add the garlic and stir-fry for 30 seconds more. Transfer to a medium saucepan.

In the same skillet over medium heat, add the tomato paste and cook for 1 minute, then add the tomato purée and deglaze, scraping up the browned bits with a wooden spoon. Transfer the tomato mixture to the saucepan with the onion and garlic.

Add the kielbasa and the beans (cooked or canned) to the saucepan, then stir in ½ cup / 120ml of the reserved liquid (if using cooked beans) or fresh water (if using canned beans), the marjoram, oregano, and ½ tsp salt. Cover and let simmer for 20 minutes.

Recipe continues

When the beans have finished simmering, in a small nonstick skillet over low heat, melt the butter. Add the flour and, while stirring vigorously, cook until it becomes lightly browned, about 2 minutes. Add a few tablespoons of the stew liquid, vigorously stir to combine, turn the heat to low, and bring to a simmer. Pour the mixture into the saucepan, while stirring constantly to combine, then stir in the cream. Let the stew simmer until thickened but still saucy, 5 to 10 minutes, then turn off the heat. Add the honey, season with salt, pepper, and additional marjoram, and stir to combine.

Ladle the hot stew into bowls and serve with hunks of fresh bread.

beans, kielbasa, onion, garlic, dried herbs, tomato paste (preserved)

When it comes to cooking, Vesemir's top of the pile. None of us can compete. Not seriously, anyway. I don't know if it's inherited talent or he owes it to years of practice, but all the meals he cooks are at least solid. His bean and sausage stew—that's my favorite. When Vesemir gets his turn in the kitchen, not even Lambert is late to the table. The real challenge is to keep Lambert from eating the damned sausage ahead of time. If the sausage survives, the stew is great. I mean, smoked meat, spices and then Vesemir's specially preserved tomato stock . . . that's the secret. Still, he needs a mound of supplies from different places to make this thing. I truly wonder how he manages to collect everything, often from villages a good way off, and bring it all to the keep each fall before the first snows.

Ciri's Breakfast Porridge

When I was a child, I recall my family making porridge using whole-grain flour for a more nutritious result. The porridge's desired thickness can be easily managed by adding more oat flakes if too liquid, or more milk if too thick. Last but not least, dried fruits and nuts provide a sweet, tart chewiness and satisfying crunch. Fruit strained from the Harviken Dried-Fruit Drink also pairs splendidly here.

—————◆ MAKES 2 SERVINGS ◆—————

1 cup / 240ml water
2 pinches kosher salt
¼ cup / 30g medium rye flour or whole-wheat flour
½ cup / 120ml whole milk
⅓ cup / 45g rolled oats
2 tsp unsalted butter
1 handful nuts (such as walnuts or hazelnuts), chopped
1 handful dried fruits (such as apricots, cranberries, or apple slices)
2 Tbsp floral honey

— — — — — ◇ — — — — —

In a small saucepan over high heat, combine the water and salt and bring to a boil. While stirring vigorously, gradually add the flour, then turn the heat to low and let simmer, stirring frequently, until the mixture is thick and starts to pull away from the sides of the pan, about 10 minutes. Add the milk and oats and continue to simmer, stirring frequently, until the oats are tender, 10 to 12 minutes. Stir in the butter and let simmer for 1 minute more. Transfer to a serving bowl, add a generous portion of chopped nuts and dried fruits, and then drizzle with the honey.

Serve the porridge immediately.

milk, oats, honey, her favorite dried fruits, and nuts

Oh gods, Ciri hated this dish. You'd think: milk, oats, some butter—what's not to like? But she refused to touch it. We could only ever convince her to eat it as a penalty for losing in our little hand-slap competitions. Thankfully, for all our sakes, somebody thought of adding a little wild honey and a handful of fruits and nuts. And so this milky mush, as unappetizing as it still looked, finally turned into something that could tempt even our stubborn little protégé . . .

Kaer Morhen Fried Mushroom Salad

lettuce, cave and mountain mushrooms, walnuts, cheese, butter

I often wonder what types of mushrooms witchers eat and what culinary properties these mushrooms possess. As I see it, the best choice for this warm salad are oyster mushrooms that turn crispy when heavily browned in a pan.

———— MAKES 1 SERVING ————

1 Tbsp / 10g nuts (such as hazelnuts or walnuts)
3½ oz / 100g oyster mushrooms
2 Tbsp vegetable oil
1 tsp unsalted butter
1 garlic clove, minced
1 pinch dried thyme
1 tsp floral honey
Kosher salt and freshly ground black pepper
1½ oz / 40g salad leaves (such as arugula, lamb's lettuce, spinach, or field greens)
⅓ cup / 30g sharp cheese (such as Cheddar or Pecorino), shaved

In a dry nonstick skillet, toast the nuts over medium-low heat, shaking the pan a few times, until slightly browned, about 2 minutes. Remove the skillet from the heat, transfer the nuts to a cutting board, let cool, and then coarsely chop.

Trim and discard the central hard stems of the mushroom clusters. If needed, brush or wipe the mushrooms with a damp kitchen towel to get rid of any dirt. Tear the larger mushrooms, using your hands, to get strips of a similar size. Arrange the mushrooms on a work surface, place a cutting board on top of them, and slightly press down to even out the thickness.

The pantry is Vesemir's mysterious kingdom. It seems organized—meticulously, obsessively, even. But the labels he's put on the neatly stacked jars, jugs and other containers are those of a mad king. Enigmatic to say the least. Quarrels about pantry mistakes break out every so often and I'm not surprised. Triss has recently grown a little wary of the salad Vesemir serves on "special" occasions. She calls some of the mushrooms from his provisions "peculiar." Now, I know Vesemir to be an experienced forager. I may be the only one apart from him to understand his classification system. So I'm sure this list of ingredients is correct. Well, mostly sure.

In a large frying pan, warm the oil, arrange the mushrooms in one layer next to each other, and fry on medium-high heat, until very browned, for 3 to 4 minutes without stirring, then flip and continue to fry on the other side, until very browned and crispy, for another 3 to 4 minutes. Lower the heat to medium-low, add the butter, garlic, and thyme and stir-fry for 1 minute. Then pour in the honey, stir to coat, and stir-fry for another 1 minute until the mushrooms are heavily caramelized and crispy. Generously season with salt and pepper and turn off the heat.

In a bowl, toss the salad leaves with the warm fried mushrooms and sprinkle with the nuts and cheese shavings. Serve immediately.

Eskel's Tvorog

This firm cottage cheese pairs well with many different spices. I oft prepare it by rolling some cheese into a ball, then coating it with nigella seeds, dried wild garlic, or crushed, colorful peppercorns. It's worth experimenting with various seasonings to find your favorite combination!

———— ◆ MAKES ABOUT 1⅓ CUPS / 300G ◆ ————

8⅓ cups / 2L buttermilk
1 tsp kosher salt

In a large pot, combine the buttermilk and salt. Set the heat to very low and slowly warm the mixture for 25 to 30 minutes, taking care not to overheat it. You should be able to comfortably put your finger in the warm buttermilk mixture. If it becomes too hot to test with your finger, reduce the heat. Gradually, curds should start to form and separate from the translucent whey. Using a spoon, gently stir the mixture a few times while heating, without breaking the curds.

When you have almost fully translucent whey, turn off the heat and set aside for 10 minutes to slightly cool. Line a fine-mesh sieve with cheesecloth and place it over a large empty pot or bowl. Then gently pour in the mixture to drain the curds. Squeeze excess water from the cheesecloth and form into a ball or disk and set aside for 2 hours at room temperature. Then transfer to the fridge, cover, and store for up to 3 days.

Eskel likes to say he's a "simple" witcher. So I see it as surprising if not downright odd that he takes the time to explore local cuisines whenever he's out on the Path. The fact is, wherever we witchers go, peasants often greet us with curses, while nobles sic their hounds on us. So when Eskel was once welcomed at a tavern with open arms, he saw it as a pleasant change. He grew plainly fond of the fresh tvorog cheese they served him. Made from buttermilk and often coated in spices, he came home calling it a "rare rural delicacy." Ever since, he has stubbornly tried to recreate it in the kitchens here, with varying degrees of success. This may be because Lambert usually stands over him, making sarcastic remarks.

Beer and Cheese Pottage

Beer pottage comes in plenty of different styles. I tasted quite a few of them as I traveled the Continent. This one, using a light beer base, adds egg yolks creamed with sugar and a pinch of ground cloves or cinnamon for a unique variation that can also be served as a dessert.

—————— ◄ MAKES 2 SERVINGS ► ——————

100g sourdough bread (such as wheat or rye)
2 cups / 480ml pale lager beer
1 pinch caraway seeds
1 Tbsp unsalted butter
3 Tbsp heavy cream
2 tsp floral honey
2 egg yolks
2 tsp granulated sugar
Tvorog (page 239), cubed or crumbled, for serving
2 pinches ground cloves for garnishing
Croutons for garnishing

– – – – – – – – ◇ – – – – – – – –

Cut off and cube the bread crust. Place the cubes of crust in a medium nonstick dry skillet over medium heat and toast until golden brown and crispy, about 2 minutes. Turn off the heat and set the croutons aside.

In a medium saucepan over very low heat, crumble the remaining crustless bread. Stir in the beer and caraway seeds and bring to a light simmer. Cook for 10 minutes, then press the mixture through a medium-mesh sieve and, using a wooden spoon, rub to press through as much of the bread as possible; discard what's left inside the sieve. Return the mixture to the pan over low heat, stir in the butter, cream, and honey and bring to a light simmer.

leftover bread, beer, butter, honey, cream, fresh crumbled tvorog

After a few dire attempts that, as Lambert put it, made us twist our mouths in disgust, we finally figured out a tasty variation on this dish that Eskel had first sampled somewhere in Caingorn. There's nothing appetizing about how this pottage looks, but this unusual combination of cooked, soft bread, beer, crumbled tvorog (use Eskel's tvorog recipe, it tastes the best), a spoonful of honey and croutons is somehow incredibly addictive!

In a small bowl, quickly whisk the egg yolks and sugar until light yellow and creamy. Add 3 Tbsp of the hot soup, whisking thoroughly. Turn off the heat and add the egg mixture to the soup, stirring constantly so the yolks don't set, until well combined.

Ladle the pottage into bowls, add a generous portion of crumbled tvorog on top, and garnish with the cloves and croutons. Serve immediately.

Lambert's Herb and Tvorog Dumplings

Fried bacon bits really make this dish sing, but a non-meat topping works just as well. Beneath the topping, it's simply unsalted butter, bread crumbs, and a pinch of salt, fried for a few minutes until golden brown and crisp, then mixed into a pile of cooked dumplings.

◄─── MAKES 2 TO 4 SERVINGS ───►

3½ oz / 100g slab bacon, cut crosswise into thin strips
9 oz / 250g Eskel's Tvorog (page 239),
  or 8 oz / 225g light cream cheese
1 egg
½ cup / 70g all-purpose flour, with more for sprinkling
Heaping 1 Tbsp potato starch
3 Tbsp chopped fresh dill
¼ cup / 15g chopped fresh flat-leaf parsley
1 tsp dried wild garlic, or dried chives
Kosher salt and freshly ground black pepper

─────◇─────

In a large nonstick skillet, combine the bacon and a splash of cold water. Set over medium heat and cook, stirring occasionally, until the water evaporates, 1 to 2 minutes, then cook until the bacon is well browned and cracklings are obtained, 7 to 10 minutes more. Turn off the heat, cover, and set aside.

In a medium bowl, using a fork, thoroughly mash the tvorog, then whisk in the egg. Add the flour, potato starch, dill, parsley, wild garlic, and ½ tsp salt, stir with the fork, then, using your hands, briefly knead just until well combined. If the dough is too sticky, sprinkle with a little flour; be careful not to add too much, since the dumplings may become too firm.

Lightly flour a work surface. Roll out the dough into a log about 8 inches / 20cm long and 1¼ inches / 3cm thick. Using a sharp knife, cut off single dumplings every ½ inch / 1.3cm.

Bring a large saucepan half full of water to a boil over medium-high heat. Turn the heat to medium, add 1 tsp salt and half the dumplings, and gently stir with a wooden spoon. Cook until the dumplings float to the surface, about 5 minutes, then turn the heat to low and let simmer until the dumplings are soft but not overdone, 2 to 3 minutes. Using a slotted spoon or spider strainer, transfer the dumplings to the skillet with the fried bacon and toss to coat in the fat. Repeat with the remaining dumplings.

Transfer the bacon and dumplings onto individual plates and sprinkle with pepper. Serve immediately.

tvorog, flour, herbs (sadly not enough), egg, salt, pepper, fried bacon

I swear, Lambert must have devised this recipe himself. I refuse to believe that any tavern out there serves this. Lambert claims he's doing us a favor, cooking the way he does. He's toughening up our stomachs, he says, thanks to which even the worst tavern fare will taste delicious. Though he lacks culinary talent entirely, Lambert is in no way discouraged. He insists, time and again, on serving us perfectly overcooked, barely edible cheese dumplings. His cooking has been the cause of many quarrels. Eskel convinced him to at least add some herbs to his signature dish. It was a start, but I've made further improvements.

Infusions

Proper herbs—they're the heart of our infusions. Sure, most are not hard to find, but for quality, you can't do much better than the southern slope by the river or the area around the mine.

  Dried and properly proportioned, some are even good as flavor enhancers. We know this because we've experimented with different blends of herbs in different liquors.

  And then there's Lambert with his "Gauntlet" — half spirit and half White Gull. Which is really just two hard liquors slapped together. Not much flavor, lots of punch.

Tales abound of the endless varieties of potions concocted by witchers, so when this journal fell into my lap, I thought I had come across a true *rara avis*. However, the fragmentary notes still visible on the pages make little sense. Yet even if they did make sense, I do not possess the knowledge to brew real potions. So instead, I've devised a culinary game that consists of recreating tasty (and yes, entirely safe) drinks based on the infusion recipes I've extracted from Coën's notes. My concoctions include a healthy tonic to replenish strength as well as a liquor for simple pleasure and relaxation. It is altogether an array of eccentric flavors loosely inspired by what many witchers carry with them on the Path.

Swallow

⟶ MAKES 1 SERVING ⟶

¼ cup / 60ml mead, or as needed

3 Tbsp 100% cranberry juice, or as needed

1 Tbsp raspberry syrup

In a large glass, combine the mead, cranberry juice, and raspberry syrup and stir to incorporate. Balance the flavor to your liking by adding more mead for sweetness or more cranberry juice for sourness.

Serve the potion immediately.

VARIATION: For an herbal version, in a teacup, combine 1 tsp dried hibiscus and ¼ cup / 60ml boiling water. Cover and let steep for 7 minutes, then strain, discarding the leaves, and set the liquid aside to cool to room temperature. Add this liquid to the potion.

dwarven spirit, ~~Coën~~ drowner brain, alcohest, ~~White Gull ingredients~~ white gull, berbercane fruit, crow's eye, ~~sulfur~~

A red potion to strengthen one's constitution.

Thunderbolt

¾ cup / 175ml pear or apple juice
½ tsp barley powder or matcha powder
1 tsp apple cider vinegar, or as needed
1 Tbsp floral honey
2 pinches kosher salt
1 thin slice fresh ginger, peeled and minced

In a large glass, combine the pear juice and barley or matcha powder. Using a small whisk, mix thoroughly, until there are no lumps remaining. Add the vinegar, honey, salt, and ginger and stir to combine. Set aside for at least 30 minutes; for a tastier drink, refrigerate the potion for 2 to 3 hours. Stir before serving.

dwarven spirit, ~~Sovereign...~~, endrega embryo, alcohest, fool's parsley leaves, white gull, verbena, ~~........~~, ~~........~~

A green tonic to elevate one's strength.

White Gull

MAKES 1 SERVING

2 Tbsp mineral or sparkling water
2 Tbsp lemon juice
1 Tbsp white elderflower syrup
¼ cup / 60ml Redanian Herbal Vodka (opposite)
Several mint leaves (optional)

In a large glass, combine the water, lemon juice, and elderflower syrup and stir to incorporate. Then stir in the vodka. If desired, roll some mint leaves between your palms and add to the drink.

Serve the potion chilled.

Redanian herbal, ~~........~~, mandrake cordial, ~~........~~
An alcoholic infusion used as a base for potions.

KAER MORHEN

Redanian Herbal Vodka

———◄ MAKES ½ CUP / 120ML ►———

Thanks to my visit to the Crow's Perch Inn in Velen, I already possessed the knowledge I needed
to understand and recreate the herbal vodka recipe that is a vital component of White Gull.

2 tsp granulated sugar
¼ cup / 60ml water
½ cup / 120ml vodka
1 small cinnamon stick
1 clove
4 caraway seeds
5 coriander seeds
1 allspice berry
1 strip of orange zest (about 1 inch / 2.5cm square)

In a small dry saucepan over medium heat, melt the
sugar. Shake the pan to evenly dissolve the sugar, then
turn the heat to low and continue to cook until the
caramel is amber, about 2 minutes. Then add the water
and simmer, stirring once or twice, until fully dissolved,
about 2 minutes. Turn off the heat and let cool to room
temperature. Transfer the mixture to an 8-ounce / 250ml
jar with a lid, add the vodka, cinnamon stick, clove,
caraway and coriander seeds, the allspice berry, and the
orange zest and stir. Tightly close the lid and infuse at
room temperature for 24 hours, shaking the jar every
6 hours. Strain the mixture and then transfer to the jar.

Store at room temperature with a lid on.

KAER MORHEN

ACKNOWLEDGMENTS

Our sincere thanks to Andrzej Sapkowski for creating the vast and multidimensional world of *The Witcher* that has so inspired us, and for honoring this book with such a grand foreword. We're also forever grateful to the CD PROJEKT RED team for believing in our vision and entrusting us with such a unique project. Our thanks to those who directly worked on this cookbook, especially: Kacper, for overseeing this project with dedication, complex help, and human-driven attitude; Borys and the localization team for perfecting language intricacies; Marcin and Przemek, for your expertise and guidance that helped us create high-quality content faithful to the universe; Alicja and Marcin, for supporting us with communication and marketing; Kinga and Bartek, for all the legal help; and Daniel, for the beautiful illustrations. Credit also should go to those who warmly welcomed us at the beginning of our story as content creators, whom we had the pleasure of working with on other projects: Paweł, MJ, Radek, Dominika, and Banan.

Thanks to Ten Speed Press and Penguin Random House for the trust, flexibility, and openness to our concepts. Shaida, we couldn't wish for a better project lead and editor, with your vast understanding toward our vision, needs, and your kind heart—our guiding light during this complex project.

Our closest friends, Jakub, Mateusz, Ola, and Aleksandra, not only contributed to this cookbook but also provided immense mental support.

To all the people within the industry who helped us in various ways along our journey and made us believe in what we do, especially Asia and Radek. Also thanks to Artur from Kaer Morhen Forge and Magda from Q-Workshop.

To Karolina's close ones and grandparents and Anita's family members, who implanted us with significant passions and supported our chosen life paths over the years.

To all the fans following our blogs and to you, dear reader, who decided to take a look at this cookbook—we hope you'll love every piece we've prepared for you inside.

We simply couldn't have made our dream come true without you all.

And finally, we're also thankful for each other—for our lively, challenging, and powerful relationship similar to that of Dandelion and Geralt: two contrasting characters, yet also complementary sidekicks and companions destined to be on a shared path to achieve bigger things together.

ABOUT THE AUTHORS

Anita Sarna and Karolina Krupecka are the creators of Witcher Kitchen (witcherkitchen.com) and Nerds' Kitchen Creations (nerdskitchencreations.com). Their main focus revolves around culinary elements in pop culture arts such as video games, books, and movies. They create real-life food recipes with photos and culinary videos, aiming to reflect the vibes of a given universe with complex scenography and visual storytelling as a tribute to and extension of the worlds designed by their original creators. Their mission is also to advocate for the importance of food motifs in creating compelling stories and believable fictional worlds, especially in video game design.

INDEX

First published in Great Britain in 2023 by Gollancz
an imprint of The Orion Publishing Group Ltd
Carmelite House, 50 Victoria Embankment
London EC4Y 0DZ

An Hachette UK Company

10 9 8 7 6 5 4 3 2 1

ISBN (HB) 978 1 399 61563 1
ISBN (eBook) 978 1 399 61564 8

Editor: Marcus Gipps
Editorial assistant: Claire Ormsby-Potter
Designer: Debbie Berne
Art Directors: Kelly Booth and Emma Campion
Production designers: Mari Gill, Faith Hague, and
Claudia Sanchez
Production manager: Dan Myers
Prepress color manager: Jane Chinn
Photo assistant and technical support: Jakub Ryfa
Prop maker: Mateusz Pieczyński
Prop custom illustrations: Aleksandra Ratajczak
Copyeditor: Dolores York
Proofreaders: Elisabeth Beller, Jacob Sammon, and
Eldes Tran
Indexer: Ken DellaPenta
Publicist: Jenna Petts
Marketer: Lucy Cameron

Printed in Italy

www.gollancz.co.uk